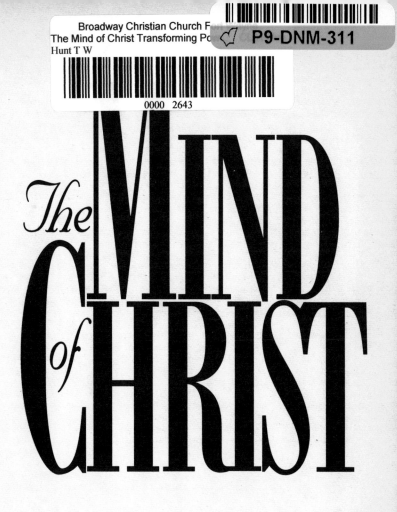

The MIND of CHRIST

This Billy Graham Evangelistic Association
special edition is published with permission
from Broadman & Holman Publishers.

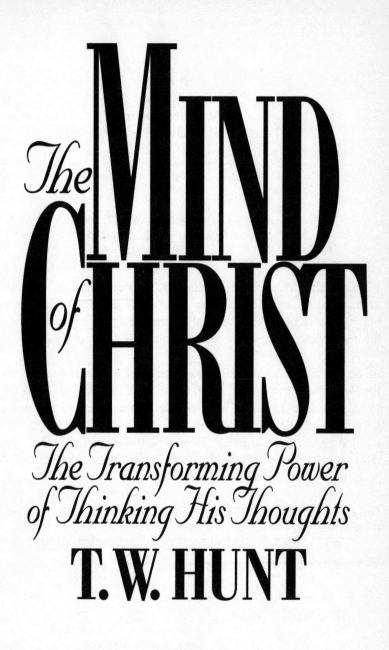

The MIND of CHRIST

The Transforming Power of Thinking His Thoughts

T. W. HUNT

BROADMAN
& HOLMAN
PUBLISHERS

Nashville, Tennessee

Dewey Decimal Classification: 248.4
Subject Heading: CHRISTIAN LIFE

Library of Congress Cataloging-in-Publication Data
Hunt, T.W. , 1929–
        The mind of Christ : the transforming power of thinking his thoughts / T.W. Hunt.
        p.   cm.
    Includes bibliographical references.
    ISBN 0-913367-83-4

    1. Jesus Christ—Example.   2. Identification (Religion)   3. Christian life—Baptist authors.   I. Title.
BT304.2.H85   1995
232.9'04—dc20

This book is dedicated to

Laverne,

who has taught me more about

the mind of Christ

than anyone else.

Acknowledgments

So many teachers, friends, and relatives have influenced my pilgrimage as I have sought the meaning of Christ-likeness that I cannot name them or even remember all of them. Among those are my parents, Tom and Ethel Hunt, who from the earliest days of my life, held up the Lord Jesus Christ as our model for living.

I will be forced to leave out large numbers of people who also helped in the preparation of this book. Dr. and Mrs. Ken Easley read an early version of this manuscript and made helpful suggestions. I feel especially indebted to my editor, Vicki Crumpton, whose ideas of organization of material were both thoughtful and useful. Vicki was also a source of real encouragement when I would become discouraged. Dr. Ernest Byers studied the medical material on the crucifixion and helped me make a number of important changes. He also made suggestions about the physical process of the crucifixion that I appropriated.

I am indebted to my son-in-law and daughter, Steve and Melana Monroe, who read the manuscript and offered timely and wise advice. They spent many hours pouring over the manuscript and suggesting important changes. I am grateful for the careful and constant help of my wife, Laverne. She read the manuscript with a fine-tooth comb and allowed no slips of the pen. I owe to her also her example of Christ-likeness. Often I have known what Christ would do by taking my cue from her!

Most of all I am indebted to the Holy Spirit who has led me in this pursuit all the way. I learned early that He glorifies Christ. He is the great enlightener who has helped me to understand what I understand of the Lord Jesus Christ.

Contents

Part 1: The Mind of Christ
1. The Mind of Christ...3
2. Christ's Freedom from Sin 17
3. Free Indeed...27
4. The Lifestyle of Christ 39

Part 2: To Be Like Christ
5. Jesus Christ, God's Son, Savior 53
6. A Servant..65
7. A Man 77
8. Humble and Obedient..91
9. Crucified...101
10. Raised from the Dead 121

Part 3: A Name Above Every Name
11. A Kingdom Above 143
12. A Kingdom Within 153

Part 4: Now and Forever, Amen
13. A Kingdom Present and to Come...................................165

Notes...173
Bibliography 181

PART ONE

The Mind of Christ

chapter one

The Mind of Christ

Let this mind be in you.

S uppose Christ broke through the veil that separates the spiritual from the physical and audibly said to you today, "I am going to require you to have My mind in all its fullness. However, I want people to know what a miracle of change I can work, so I am going to reveal to your church what your mind is like right now. Next Sunday, in your church, I am going to take over the morning service and play back for all to hear every thought you had this last week." Would it appall you or delight you if Christ revealed your thoughts?

We unconsciously assume that our outer, physical, visible actions are going to be the basis for our judgment. In the Bible, though, God places the emphasis on the inner, invisible actions of the mind.

You may protest that you have never committed adultery (for example). Yet Jesus said, "But I say to you, that everyone who looks on a woman to lust for her has committed adultery with her already in his heart" (Matt. 5:28). You would have a horror of the thought of murder, but Jesus warned, "But I say to you that everyone who is angry with his brother shall be guilty before the court" (Matt. 5:22). He equated the sin of anger with that of murder. Ahab's greed (1 Kings 21:1–6), a mental sin, preceded the stealing of Naboth's vineyard. (Although it was Jezebel who carried out Naboth's murder, the entire sordid episode started with Ahab's greed; see 1 Kings 21:15–16.) Cain's inner anger and jealousy

(Gen. 4:5) anchored in his mind before the outward act of murder (Gen. 4:8). Martha's mental sin of anxiety led to the visible sin of quarreling (Luke 10:38–41).

The mind has always been more important to God than our outward actions. In the Old Testament, the emphasis was on the heart. At times, the Bible uses the word *heart* where we would use the word *mind*, as in the injunction, "Apply your heart to discipline" (Prov. 23:12). In the New Testament, Jesus used the word *heart* in the same sense: "And Jesus knowing their thoughts said, 'Why are you thinking evil in your hearts?'" (Matt. 9:4).

Most of us, most of the time, are satisfied if we satisfy the expectations of society and the requirements of God by our outer, visible actions. God looks on the inner; He said, as early as Samuel's day, that "man looks at the outward appearance, but the LORD looks at the heart" (1 Sam. 16:7). In the more restricted emphasis of the New Testament, we can say "the Lord looks at the mind."

Have you ever evaluated the condition of your mind? Below is an inventory of two opposing sets of mental states. This evaluation is only for your information. Do it in absolute privacy, with no one but the Lord and you knowing your performance at this stage. You will not score the exercise. Its sole purpose is to help you know what your mind is like at present.

As you prayerfully study each item, place a mental mark on the line in the center where you think you would be today. If you believe you would incline toward the left most of the time, determine how far to the left you would be. If you incline toward the right, note where on the line you are. You may find yourself on the left on some items and to the right on others, or even in the middle.

Evaluation of Your Current Mental State

Jealousy or envy	Rejoicing in the success of your brother or sister in Christ
Wanting to get even	Praying for enemies
Bitterness toward God	Acceptance of God's will
Bitterness toward others	Generosity toward others
Sexual lust	Holiness of thought
Lust for position or power	Humility toward others

Hatred of someone	_____	Love of enemy
Anger	_____	Being peaceable
Resentment	_____	Forgiving
Pride in your station in life	_____	Humility before God
Pride in your ability or looks	_____	Not self-centered
Looking down on others	_____	Reverencing God's work in others
Self-love	_____	Selfless love of others
Self-seeking	_____	Seeking the kingdom
Slandering others	_____	Encouraging others
Reliance on self	_____	Reliance on God
Boasting	_____	Pointing to the achievements of others
Unthankful to God	_____	Always thankful to God
Lazy	_____	Hard-working
Undisciplined	_____	Disciplined
Headstrong	_____	Willing to yield to others
Addicted to television	_____	Devoted to prayer
Hunger for things of the world	_____	Hunger for God
Combative, contentious	_____	Yielding personal rights
Compromising	_____	Faithful
Ambitious for self or for family	_____	Ambitious for others
Tendency to lie or pervert truth	_____	Telling the truth even when it hurts
Attention usually focused on the world	_____	Attention usually focused on God

Do you like the current condition of your mind? More importantly, would God like the state of your mind right now? What if it were possible to have a mind like Christ's?

Why Is Having the Mind of Christ Important for Believers?

The Old Testament places little emphasis on our becoming like God while the New Testament reiterates numerous injunctions to imitate God or to be like Christ. In its earliest pages, the Bible tells us that God created us in His image (Gen. 1:26–27; 5:1). Yet after Adam's fall, the Old

Testament has very little reference to our likeness to God and no admonitions to become like Him.

The Old Testament emphasis is on the *difference* between God and man. "'For My thoughts are not your thoughts, Neither are your ways My ways,' declares the LORD. 'For as the heavens are higher than the earth, So are My ways higher than your ways, And My thoughts than your thoughts'" (Isa. 55:8–9). Apart from Christ, our ways today are not His ways. The Old Testament idea was that God molds us and shapes us from the outside: "We are the clay, and Thou our potter; And all of us are the work of Thy hand" (Isa. 64:8).

The New Testament makes a radical shift in its emphasis. Here God in Christ is made like us: "Since then the children share in flesh and blood, He Himself likewise also partook of the same. . . . Therefore, He had to be made like His brethren in all things, that He might become a merciful and faithful high priest in things pertaining to God" (Heb. 2:14, 17).

After redemption was accomplished, the New Testament picks up the theme from the opening chapters of the Bible, and once more we are to be like God. Paul said, "Put on the new self, *created to be like God* in true righteousness and holiness" (Eph. 4:24 NIV, emphasis added). The purpose of the new self is Godlikeness. He told the Colossians, "[You] have put on the new self, which is being renewed in knowledge *in the image of its Creator*" (Col. 3:10 NIV, emphasis added). In redemption, we are again in the image of God.

During His earthly days, even before the mighty work of redemption, Jesus said, "It is enough for the disciple that he become as his teacher, and the slave as his master" (Matt. 10:25). Specifically, we are now to be like Jesus, who was God made human. He became like us so that we might become like Him. "For whom He foreknew, He also predestined to become conformed to the image of His Son, that He might be the first-born among many brethren" (Rom. 8:29). John sees an apocalyptic end of the process: "But we know that when he appears, we shall be like him, because we shall see him just as he is" (1 John 3:2 NIV).

Jesus Himself invites us, "Take My yoke upon you, and learn from Me" (Matt. 11:29). He went from birth to death living our kind of life to give us an example of what God meant man to be. He suffered our kind of temptations (Heb. 4:15). He knew the pangs of hunger, thirst, exhaustion, denial, and betrayal by friends. And in all of that, He invites us to learn from Him.

To help us learn, He gave Himself as our example. To help us learn servanthood, He washed the disciples' feet. Afterward, He told them, "For I gave you an example that you also should do as I did to you" (John 13:15). In the same way, "Christ also suffered for you, leaving you an example for you to follow in His steps" (1 Pet. 2:21). We are to love because that is the example of Christ. Paul told the Ephesians, "And walk in love, just as Christ also loved you, and gave Himself up for us, an offering and a sacrifice to God as a fragrant aroma" (Eph. 5:2).

Philippians 2:5 tells us that we are to have the mind of Christ. This verse is part of a poem (Phil. 2:5–11) that was originally a hymn.[1] This verse says that we are to think like Jesus thinks. In the original Greek, the command is in the form of the verb *phroneite,* the plural imperative of the verb *phroneo,* "to think or to be minded in a certain way." Our mind is to have the same characteristics that Christ's mind has.

The astonishing purpose of the Father was to bring many children into the perfect image of His glorious Son. The New Testament reflects that emphasis frequently.

Jesus told a parable about how God works in process: "The kingdom of God is like a man who casts seed upon the soil; and goes to bed at night and gets up by day, and the seed sprouts up and grows—how, he himself does not know. The soil produces crops by itself; first the blade, then the head, then the mature grain in the head. But when the crop permits, he immediately puts in the sickle, because the harvest has come" (Mark 4:26–29). The spiritual mind will develop in the same way that a little child's mind develops. Even at spiritual birth, we have the "mind of Christ" (1 Cor. 2:16), but in subsequent growth that mind must contend with established habits, the culture in which we live, and the work of Satan. In us, the mind of Christ matures in a process of growth.

Several passages in the New Testament suggest that the process of our conforming to Christ's image is primarily the work of God (for example, John 15:16; Phil. 2:13). We are the subjects, and God is the active agent. Paul wrote of this perfection as being accomplished in process: "But we all, with unveiled face beholding as in a mirror the glory of the Lord, are being transformed into the same image from glory to glory, just as from the Lord, the Spirit" (2 Cor. 3:18). Our destiny is to be like Christ. God intends it, and the Scripture directs us to participate in the process of becoming like Him.

Since Christ is divine, we humans cannot be like Him in *all* ways. We cannot imitate His omnipotence, omnipresence, omniscience, infinity, immutability, and the attributes peculiar to divinity. On the other hand, in the limitation of His incarnation He did demonstrate specific qualities that we also have in our new nature. We can grow in these qualities: mercy, love, long-suffering, and even holiness and grace. We have to look to those humanly manifested qualities that He expects us to imitate. They are indeed also divine attributes, but they constitute that part of God's nature that He invested in redeemed humanity.

What Is God's Standard for the Mind?

Six times the New Testament describes or implies what the Christian's mind is to be like. In each case the passage mentions the word *mind*. From these we can derive six adjectives that describe God's ideal for the mind. As you read what the New Testament says about the mind, check your mind to see if these adjectives describe you.

Alive

The first description occurs in Romans 8:6: "For the mind set on the flesh is death, but the mind set on the Spirit is *life* and peace" (emphasis added).

Our first adjective is *alive*. Harold L. heard me teach the seminar "The Mind of Christ" and made an appointment with me. He was not sure that he really had spiritual life like I was describing. He had made a profession of faith in Christ as a child, but he didn't understand what it meant. He told me, "No change came into my life then. The same sins persisted, and my commitment was entirely perfunctory. I made my profession to please others."

Genuine conversion means a change of life and especially a change with our attitude toward sin. As we talked, it became clear that Harold had not understood that he would have a different attitude toward sin after conversion. Knowing that life in Christ produces a new kind of consciousness of holiness and unholiness, I asked him how he felt when he sinned. He confessed that he had not known sorrow for sins, only regret. Real repentance involves sharing the grief of God over our sin. This turned out to be the first indication he had ever had that life in Christ makes a real difference.

He returned on another day and told me, "I am sure that I do not have the life you are describing." Under the prompting of the Spirit, I asked him if he would be willing to forsake his life of sin to accept Christ. He was thoughtful as he said, "I want the life of Christ you are describing. Yes, I will forsake my sins." He bowed in prayer, and I led him through a commitment to Christ.

Believers know that we are dead without Christ and have everlasting life in Him, but Jesus went further than saying we have mere existence: He said that He came so that we might have *abundant* life (John 10:10). We show this life (or death) constantly by the choices we make.

The mind that is alive chooses the spiritual rather than the fleshly. For example, take our thought life. The world sends a constant barrage of messages to us—politics, world, business, sex, sports, products, and others. God also is sending us messages, messages about His expressed will in the Bible for us, promptings about words to say or not to say, anger to control, or patience to extend.

Our minds are cluttered with information. They race from subject to subject. We can receive these various messages indiscriminately, we can reject some, and dwell on others. Many people choose to follow vacantly the current track of messages coming in, regardless of their source. On the other hand, we can reject some of them or even cut off their source (such as television).

Jesus chose to think about "His Father's business." Satan tried to entice Him to turn stones into bread in the wilderness temptation. In a moment of extreme physical weakness, exhausted and desperately hungry, Jesus made a choice. He said, "It is written, 'Man shall not live on bread alone, but on every word that proceeds out of the mouth of God'" (Matt. 4:4). In His choice, He demonstrated that abundant spiritual life can overrule and dominate even when the flesh cries most desperately for satisfaction. Do you have this kind of spiritual life?

Peaceful

Romans 8:6 gives us another adjective to apply to the spiritual mind: "The mind set on the Spirit is life and peace." The spiritual mind is peaceful. Paul had said in the previous verse, "Those who are according to the flesh set their minds on the things of the flesh, but those who are according to the Spirit, the things of the Spirit" (Rom. 8:5). Note again that we *set* our minds. Peace is a fruit, not an attainment. Our work is setting the mind; God's work is the peace.

Sin separates us from God, the source of peace. The Bible tells us, "Your iniquities have made a separation between you and your God" (Isa. 59:2). Jesus wept over Jerusalem and said, "If you had known in this day, even you, the things which make for peace! But now they have been hidden from your eyes" (Luke 19:42). He would have been the source of their peace.

Jesus had peace. His life was completely free from sin and the ravages of the world system. He promised rest to the weary and burdened (Matt. 11:28). We find rest by taking His yoke. Tell Him now that you are willing to take that yoke.

Single-minded

Second Corinthians 11:3 provides a third adjective that describes the mind: "But I am afraid, lest as the serpent deceived Eve by his craftiness, your minds should be led astray from the simplicity and purity of devotion to Christ." Paul is telling us that the mind of Christ is single-minded.

While we live in this world, one of our perplexing problems is becoming distracted, or, as Paul says, being "led astray." Our minds dart off in hundreds of directions during the course of a day. Every student knows that the discipline of attention is an achievement; normally it comes with years of experience.

Jesus' entire life is a flawless example of single-mindedness. When Peter tried to turn Him away from the cross, He rebuked Peter sternly (Matt. 16:23). When He "resolutely set His face to go to Jerusalem" (that is, for the cross, Luke 9:51), He was single-minded. At the end of His life, He said that He had completed the work God gave Him to do (John 17:4). From beginning to end, nothing could deflect Him from God's purposes. Are you like that?

Lowly

Paul gives another description of the godly mind in Philippians 2:3: "Let nothing be done through strife or vainglory; but in lowliness of mind let each esteem other better than themselves" (KJV). The mind is to be lowly. Believers cannot be humble unless they are lowly; humility follows lowliness of mind. Humility speaks of a relationship to others and to God; lowliness is a state of mind.

We can foster lowliness by concentrating on a genuine appreciation for the person of God. We start there. It gives us perspective. For years I have kept notebooks on the attributes of God and His names. I begin my quiet time every morning by meditating on the attributes of God. I never quite feel prepared to approach God in prayer for the immense work of His kingdom until I find myself in a state of reverence and awe before Him.

Those who met God in the Bible always first experienced genuine terror before Him. This is a godly fear, as opposed to carnal fear. In the Bible those who met God did not need to be convinced of the need for lowliness.

If we were to write a script for how the Son of God would appear, we would not have cast Him as a carpenter. Note whom He chose for friends—fishermen, tax collectors, common people. He submitted to a criminal's death. He was lowly. Pray to have this quality in your life.

Pure

Paul speaks about the mind in Titus 1:15: "To the pure, all things are pure; but to those who are defiled and unbelieving, nothing is pure, but both their mind and their conscience are defiled." Here purity is described as the natural state of the Christian. Impurity is reached by corruption.

In our times, the "natural" spiritual state, or being filled with God's Spirit and growing in Christ, is harder to maintain for several reasons. The first is the constant assault of information on our beleaguered senses. Tempters have always abounded, but they now have resources within our environment to take us into unprecedented realms of sin.

The impurity Christians battle today touches primarily two areas. The first is the lust for the forbidden, expressed as a preoccupation with anything unlawful—wrongful sex, horoscopes, soap operas, and other lusts—in short, the desire to express oneself outside the realm of normal Christian activity. The second is the lust for power, expressed either in lust for wealth or for position.

No one ever overcame either of these kinds of lusts without preparation. Purity demands that we know ahead of time what we will do when temptation comes. The ordinary Christian will probably not make a spiritual decision under the duress of temptation. If we understood the dread abyss that temptation itself is, we would cry, as Jesus told us to, "Lead us not into temptation." Satan knows how to introduce temptation into a moment of weakness.

Our safest course is to avoid temptation entirely, but our culture has made that difficult. Strength comes before, not during, temptation. Overcoming is a prior act. Know ahead of time which lusts are your greatest weaknesses. For some lusts you must be prepared to avert your eyes. Others may require that you quote appropriate Scripture. Have certain Scriptures memorized and ready. For other lusts you may go immediately to prayer. Are you prepared before temptation comes?

Sensitive and Responsive

When Jesus appeared to the disciples on the evening of the resurrection, "He opened their minds to understand the Scriptures" (Luke 24:45). When He chose the disciples He had recognized in them a quality that made them fit subjects for three and a half years of intensive training. The disciples did not always learn quickly, but they were teachable (as a teacher I have found many students teachable who were slow to comprehend). They at least wanted to learn. They were responsive.

The adjective *responsive* implies a spiritual sensitivity to God. This responsiveness is a sensitivity that recognizes the distinguishing fingerprint of God. The disciples were sensitive when they asked, "Lord, teach us to pray" (Luke 11:1). In this petition, they were not merely envying the ability of Jesus to perform miracles (earlier He had given them authority to heal the sick and cast out demons). Jesus was intensely spiritual, and they wanted that quality of profound spirituality in their own lives.

This quality—responsiveness to God—is indispensable for progress in the spiritual life. We need for God's Spirit to sensitize us to Himself. How can we cultivate that sensitivity? One way is to give God a chance by dwelling in His Word. Specifically, what Jesus "opened their minds" to was Scripture. He wants us to understand His word, and we cannot understand it if we do not spend time meditating on it. Prayer also sensitizes the spirit. When the disciples wanted to imitate Him, it was His teaching on prayer that they requested.

Jesus was sensitive to His Father in the utmost degree. He said, "I do nothing on My own initiative, but I speak these things as the Father taught Me" (John 8:28). He claimed to *see* what the Father was doing, to *hear* what the Father was saying, and to *do* nothing independently of the Father. He devoted Himself to reflecting the mind of the Father, and His reflection was exact.

As the Father is to the Son, so Christ is to us. He imitated the Father; we imitate Christ. He saw the activity of the Father; we pay close attention to the known earthly activity of Jesus (and, for that matter, also to His present activity). He heard from the Father; we must hear from Him. The Father taught Him; He teaches us. He could do nothing independently of the Father; we cannot function independently of Him. He was very close to the Father; we must remain close to Him. Pray that God will make you more sensitive to Him.

What Principles Govern the Three Actions That God Has Commanded Us to Take with Our Mind?

The New Testament gives three specific commands—imperative verbs —that concern the mind. These scriptural mandates give us the clues necessary to discern how to think in the same way that Christ thought. The three commands can be classified as the beginning, middle, and ending stages of a process that culminates in spiritual maturity.

The Will Principle

The first principle, or the beginning of the process, is found in Colossians 3:2: "Set your mind on the things above, not on the things that are on earth." Paul is stating a principle—the Will Principle. We must set our mind. Many decisions that could be difficult or confusing in the heat of an emotional or complex situation can be simplified by starting with this command.

The opposite of will is instinct (by instinct I mean unwilled reactions). Major or life-changing decisions are not a problem with animals. With human beings, the will is that part of our mind over which we have control. "We are taking every thought captive to the obedience of Christ" (2 Cor. 10:5). The will enables us to obey in spite of feeling. Often we cannot control our emotions, but we always have control over the will. Our identification with Christ must begin here or not at all.

This verb *set* comes first because Christ identified His will with that of His Father repeatedly. In the last week of His earthly life, as He faced the cross, He said (when some Greeks came to Him), "Now My soul has become troubled; and what shall I say, 'Father, save Me from this hour'? But for this purpose I came to this hour. Father, glorify Thy name" (John 12:27–28). He openly confessed that His emotions were one place, but His will was another. Every Christian is familiar with His determined plea in Gethsemane, "Yet not what I will, but what Thou wilt" (Mark 14:36). Jesus' performance was impeccable because He had set His will from the beginning.

When we set our will and become like Christ, God will purify our resolve. I was once asked to take a position that would involve both personal sacrifice and a large salary cut. It also offered an opportunity to expand God's kingdom in a way that nothing else offered. My feelings said no, but my will chose the will of God. Only the will can choose beyond feelings.

The River Principle

The second New Testament verb, or command, that is used with the word *mind* is in Romans 12:2: "Be transformed by the renewing of your mind." The Christian actually lives in a constant state of renewal! After we give our will to God, we must continue this process.

In the command to be transformed by the renewing of our mind, we have another principle—the River Principle. Our growth is like the flow of a river. Jesus said, "He who believes in Me, as the Scripture said, 'From his innermost being shall flow rivers of living water'" (John 7:38). Our problem is that most of us do not work on the River Principle, we work on the Pond Principle. Ponds stagnate, but rivers flow. Ponds become puddles, but rivers become oceans. We are to grow, and our growth is to be God-sized. Even Jesus grew: "And Jesus kept increasing in wisdom and stature, and in favor with God and men" (Luke 2:52).

The body grows by producing new cells. That newness is a sign of life. Failure to produce newness is a sign of death. A constant renewing is also to characterize the spiritual life. An organism that is not renewing itself is dying. The same principle applies to our spiritual lives.

I have learned to expect spiritual newness. The form of the newness no longer surprises me. Sometimes the newness comes in the shape of new insights. It may come in the form of spiritual energy. At times it is a new and deeper meaning applied to an old familiar verse. Newness may occur as we move into a deeper relationship to the body of Christ or to another Christian. It may involve a commitment of some kind. On other occasions newness takes the form of a renewed strength or a different way to resist temptation. The expression of newness cannot be exhausted or God would not be creative. The river flows. Newness is the way of progress; we are moving from one glory to another (2 Cor. 3:18).

The Readiness Principle

Our third verb-command associated with the mind takes us to the climax of the process: "Gird your minds for action" (1 Pet. 1:13). In the first century, people wore long, flowing robes. To run or move quickly, a person had to turn the robe into a kind of pantaloon by "girding up" the robe.

This illustrates the Readiness Principle. Our minds are to remain prepared for action. Jesus remained alert, or ready, as various groups tried to trap Him with trick questions in Luke 20:20–40. The "scribes and the chief priests" asked whether Jews should pay taxes to the foreign

Roman government. Their trap failed as He answered that they should satisfy both God and Caesar appropriately. When the Sadducees questioned Him about resurrection, He deftly corrected their erroneous ideas about the nature of the future life.

Readiness is being qualified for service. If our will is set and our mind has grown through constant renewal, we will be qualified for any test God allows to come our way.

The Practical Development of the Mind of Christ

Throughout the process of learning to think the thoughts of Christ, our mind will progressively assume the qualities of His mind. Below is a guide to the kind of outlook we will have if we develop these qualities. Start now trying to affirm the propositions on the right.

Adjectives	Indications of Continuing Growth
Alive	1. My conscience always responds quickly to the Holy Spirit.
	2. I am becoming more conscious of God throughout the day.
Peaceful	3. The joy and peace of Christ are replacing fleshly joys and mental conflicts.
	4. I accept the circumstances of my life as being a tool of God.
Single-minded	5. I always consult the Lord when I make a decision.
	6. I am learning new things about the Lord regularly that strengthen and confirm the earlier, basic concepts I started with.
Lowly	7. I am growing more humble before God and before others.
	8. I am growing less ambitious for self, more ambitious for the kingdom.
Pure	9. I interpret my circumstances in the realization that God is always with me.
	10. I know that God works every day, and I recognize the hand of God in my life quickly.
	11. I am developing a stronger desire not to sin.
Responsive	12. I am growing in my thirst for God.
	13. I am growing in my faith in God.
	14. I respond immediately when God speaks to me.

15. I read and memorize the Bible.
16. I spend time in prayer daily.

What do you do with those propositions you cannot now affirm? *You* do nothing. Only God can change you. God is more anxious for you to have the mind of Christ than you are. Tell God you are willing for Him to change you. He will do what you ask, because conforming you to the image of Christ is His will.

We are to obey these commands then if we are to follow the New Testament exhortations about the mind—set our mind, renew our mind, and gird up our mind. In doing them, we are imitating the example of Christ. As you progress through this book, much of the time you will be engaging in one of these mental operations.

Scripture shows us six qualities our mind is to have. We are to be alive, peaceful, single-minded, lowly, pure, and responsive. In doing so, we are obeying the Scripture and becoming like Christ.

Conclusion

God's goal for me is that I be like Christ. The one aspect of my personality that He will constantly measure for Christlikeness is my mind. He helps in my growth by revealing through His word the expectations He has for my mind. I am assured that I can have His mind because of His office as Savior. Through His word, His work, His grace, and His Spirit, I have the mind of Christ and will grow in it.

chapter two

Christ's Freedom from Sin

Let this mind be in you.

*U*nholy persons cannot think holy thoughts. The first step in having the mind of Christ is to be set free from sin, even unconscious sin. Many believers have unconscious areas of bondage to sin in their lives. So long as sin has control over any area of our mind, we are in bondage in that area. "Sin shall not be master over you" (Rom. 6:14).

Positionally, the Christian is free from bondage to sin. Because of his position, he need not be enslaved to sin. This is not only a matter of fact (our position in Christ) but of responsibility. Practically though, Satan has certain areas in which he works unceasingly on our thought patterns. Usually we are unconscious of our bondage in these areas. No Christian will become free of sin in this life, but we can be free from bondage. My first discovery of the possibility of repatterning my mind to become free of bondage came almost as a surprise.

It was a Saturday in August 1972. I had memorized the Book of James and was spending that morning meditating on James 3:13–4:3. I was alone; my wife had gone to the beauty shop and my daughter was attending orchestra practice.

Qualities of Wisdom

James says:

"Who is a wise man and endued with knowledge among you? Let him show out of a good conversation his works with meekness of wisdom. But if ye have bitter envying and strife in your hearts, glory not, and lie not against the truth. This wisdom descendeth not from above, but is earthly, sensual, devilish. For where envying and strife is, there is confusion and every evil work. But the wisdom that is from above is first pure, then peaceable, gentle, and easy to be entreated, full of mercy and good fruits, without partiality [this could also mean without wavering], and without hypocrisy" (James 3:13–17 KJV).

The eight virtues in verse 17 begin with purity and end with sincerity:

> pure
> peaceable
> gentle
> entreatable (or approachable)
> merciful
> fruitful
> steadfast (without partiality or without wavering)
> sincere (without hypocrisy)

Actually, these eight virtues are a partial picture of the mind of Christ. He was pure, peaceable, gentle, entreatable, and all these qualities. He was perfect in each one.

James continues,

"And the fruit of righteousness is sown in peace of them that make peace. From whence come wars and fightings among you? come they not hence, even of your lusts that war in your members? Ye lust, and have not: ye kill, and desire to have, and cannot obtain: ye fight and war, yet ye have not, because ye ask not. Ye ask, and receive not, because ye ask amiss, that ye may consume it upon your lusts" (James 3:18–4:3 KJV)

As I was contemplating these words, I stumbled onto an insight that had eluded me earlier. I saw that James was saying that my lusts (the Greek word can mean "pleasures" or "passions") would create war or conflict within me.

Conflict Within

I decided to put that concept to an immediate practical test. I would write down all my wants, or passions, good and bad, and try to discern if indeed they actually *acted on one another*. On a legal-sized pad I began to list my desires in a vertical column with no particular regard for priority, but simply as they occurred to me. I also determined to be scrupulously honest before the Lord in making this inventory, and then burn it before anyone came home!

The first desire I wrote down was "a new suit." Then I wrote "a washer and dryer" because at that time we had been four years without either and had found the washateria very inconvenient at times. The third desire I wrote down (and I am chagrined to say it was not the first) was that I wanted students and faculty to honor the name of the Lord Jesus Christ on the seminary campus where I was teaching at that time. I will not tell you what the fourth item on the list was, but I will tell you that resisting it was like trying to resist an itch. Satan knows that if he can get our attention for five seconds, he may have our mind for five minutes!

The fifth desire I wrote down was a desire for a certain personal quality in my life. I had a friend who had been through a series of trials. Through these trials he remained consistent, that is, he was not up or down as the trials should have carried him, but remained faithful to the Lord regardless of the circumstances. At that time I was experiencing a series of ups and downs in my life. I wanted the quality of consistent faith, like that of my friend, so I added that as a desire to the list.

My sixth desire, like my first and second, was for a material object. I thought that I had settled the issue of materialism. That morning, though, under the leadership of the Holy Spirit, trying to be honest with God alone, I found that there were yet many *things* that I wanted.

And so it went. I filled the page with desires or lusts, mixing the good with the bad, listing them as they occurred to me. That is how the lusts came to my mind, indiscriminately, without regard to order or to goodness or to badness. In other words, I had a picture of how my mind normally worked.

In what way did these passions "war with one another"? My fourth desire had been an unholy itch, unwelcome but often present. My third desire, on the other hand, was a desire that honor come to Christ. Between the unholy itch and the desire to honor Christ was a conflict! I truly wanted to honor the Lord but sometimes violated that very desire by allowing an opposite, conflicting desire to surface. One lust really acted on the other!

Next I realized that the reason my faith was not consistent (my fifth desire) was that I had not really resolved the issue of materialism. Again, one desire created friction with another. I was a divided person. Some of my wants or lusts actively opposed the others. Too often, if I made a choice concerning what to think about, the lower won over the higher. My choices concerning what to think about were themselves thoughtless. That is to say, I had spent most of my life unconscious of the process of thinking. So little of my thinking was controlled by my will. The Bible was right. My passions were conflicting in my mind, that is, within me.

The Wholeness of Christ

When I realized this conflict, my mind turned back to the eight qualities of wisdom in James 3:17 and what Christ's mind was like. What did He desire? His earliest recorded words were spoken at the age of twelve: "I must be about my Father's business." The "must" is an indication of strong desire. Eighteen years later, just before beginning His great Galilean ministry, He told His disciples, "My food is to do the will of Him who sent Me, and to accomplish His work" (John 4:34). After a long passage of time, He still had that same desire to be about "His Father's business." About two years after this, near the end of the Galilean ministry, He said that He came down from heaven "not to do My own will, but the will of Him who sent Me" (John 6:38). This one desire had dominated His passions from at least His twelfth year, through the beginning of His ministry at age thirty, and even at about age thirty-two.

At the end of His life, the night before He died, He prayed, "I glorified Thee on the earth, having accomplished the work which Thou hast given Me to do" (John 17:4). To the very end, He was concerned primarily with "His Father's business." That one desire—the desire to do the work of His Father—persisted as the dominant passion of His life from His childhood, through His maturity, and found perfect realization in His death. Jesus had no unholy want; His one overriding desire controlled His thoughts.

On the other hand, my desires (plural) formed a confused, inconsistent, and disordered picture. Christ was a glorious, integrated whole. Some of my desires were hostile, even foreign, to other desires. And yet, as a Christian, earlier I had deliberately placed my life at the disposition of the Holy Spirit. Now He was taking me deeper by introducing a concern about thought itself. He was leading me to understand the importance of placing my conscious thought-life at His disposal.

The virtues in James 3:17 do not describe all the mind of Christ, but they describe important parts of it. It occurred to me: What if I were like James 3:17—pure as Christ is, peaceable, gentle, and all these qualities of wisdom? Do any of those qualities conflict with any of the others? Look at them for yourself. Does purity ever conflict with peace? Or peace with gentleness, or entreatability with mercy, or fruitfulness with sincerity? Do these qualities clash with one another or do they blend and harmonize?

The sobering yet wondrous fact is that in the eight qualities of this verse, we have perfect integration. All these qualities work *with,* and not *against,* one another. Each works on behalf of the others; they enhance one another.

Christ really was a grand concord. He had an integrated mind. He only had one great passion, and all His attributes work hand-in-glove with one another. Each of His qualities complement and help one another. His purity can but result in peace. His peace makes His gentleness more winsome. He is a true whole and, in fact, the only true whole in history. He is unmixed; nothing in Him contradicts anything else in His mind or His personality. All in Him is integrated and all is unity.

He is also complete, lacking nothing. Sometimes we speak from one isolated aspect of our personality. Every statement by Christ comes from His completeness. In that fullness, everything He says must be true, as He is truth. His truth is absolute, and He cannot express untruth because He is whole. The whole of Him contains nothing foreign, no unessential or distracting quality. All the attributes of Christ exist together in perfect rapport. In that perfection, He is indivisible. All parts adhere; He is perfect unity.

How Do the Qualities of Wisdom Work with the Fruit of the Spirit?

Earlier in my life the Lord graciously granted me a profound renewal of spiritual life. During this fresh work in my life I wanted God to work out the nine qualities in Galatians 5:22–23 that are the fruit of the Spirit. Jesus is God, but the Holy Spirit is God also, and whatever the Spirit produces should show the same kind of integration and wholeness that

Christ Himself had. I wrote down the nine qualities that are the fruit of the Spirit:

> love
> joy
> peace
> long-suffering
> gentleness
> goodness
> faith
> meekness
> temperance

Then I inspected these qualities to see if they worked together as harmoniously as those of wisdom in James 3:17. Does love make war against joy or does it produce joy? Do peace and gentleness give a harsh discord or do they work together? All the qualities in this verse reciprocate well. Each complements and even *increases* the power of the others. They form a symphony, perfect in unity. No one of them distracts from the glory of another; the composite is glorious in its integration and unity.

Now I had two sets of biblical qualities, each complete in itself for the purpose of its own context, and each having perfect unity within itself:

Wisdom in James 3:17 (adjectives)	Fruit of the Spirit in Galatians 5:22–23 (nouns)
pure	love
peaceable	joy
gentle	peace
entreatable	long-suffering
merciful	gentleness
fruitful	goodness
steadfast	faith
sincere	meekness
	temperance

Though they harmonize within themselves, I wondered if the two sets harmonized with one another. The virtues in James are all adjectives, and those in Galatians are all nouns. I decided to apply each adjective from James to the nouns from Galatians to see if the combinations made sense. Does it make sense to talk about a "pure love"? Indeed it does. You may also talk about a "fruitful goodness" or a "steadfast faith." The descriptions "peaceful love," "gentle love," or "entreatable love" are apt. The combined lists show all kinds of possible and reasonable combinations: merciful gentleness, fruitful faith, or any combination you like.

Let us reverse the process by turning all the adjectives into nouns and all the nouns into adjectives with combinations like "loving purity," "lovingly purifying," "peaceful gentleness," "long-suffering mercy," "faithful sincerity," and so on. Regardless of the direction, the two lists work perfectly together.

I saw now that the mind of Christ is an integrated mind in which each quality works perfectly with every other quality. In fact, the qualities enhance one another. The mind of Christ has no inner conflicts. I looked again at the conflicts on my list of desires and felt helpless against the itches and the materialism that honesty before God had revealed. God knew it all along and now I knew it. But how could I change it? We speak lightly of changing our mind, but what if you really had to change the *qualities* of your mind?

I felt entrapped by my weaknesses. According to Romans 6:14, sin is not to have dominion, "for you are not under law, but under grace." Freedom from bondage to sin is not accomplished by will power, but by the grace of the Holy Spirit. I took the list of my desires, knelt, held it up toward heaven, and cried to the Lord, "Lord, what I need is to get my 'wanter' fixed. In my own strength, I am captive to my own lusts. But I am under grace. In Jesus' name, I ask You to 'fix my wanter.'" I then added, "And in Jesus' name, I free You to do anything You have to do to 'fix my wanter.' I will not quarrel with any procedure You consider necessary. I know that You really do want me to be like Jesus, regardless of the cost."

A Greater Obsession

I had intended to destroy the list. But facing one of the greatest challenges of my Christian growth, I felt I could not do it alone. When my wife, Laverne, returned that morning, I shared with her the insights from my study and the prayer I had prayed. I asked her to pray with me that God would completely free me from the mastery of any sin in my mind as a step in achieving integration of mind.

The Lord immediately began a process of answering that prayer. To accomplish His purpose, He began using a single verse, Matthew 6:33: "Seek first His [God's] kingdom and His righteousness." The Holy Spirit haunted me with that verse night and day. It echoed constantly, like a refrain, in the back of my mind. If I got into an argument, the Spirit would remind me of my greater seeking. If an unholy lust popped into my mind, I found myself turning quickly to seek God's righteousness.

Romans 12:2 commands us to be "transformed by the renewing of your mind." This was precisely what was happening to me. In myself I could not change my mind, but God the Spirit knew how to give me a *greater obsession.* Developing a greater obsession is the key to freedom from the dominion of sin. God was transforming my self-seeking into seeking His kingdom and righteousness. By the end of the fall, I was conscious of a complete renewal of my mind in the area of my wants. At long last, the major part of my attention was devoted to bringing Christ's kingdom.

However, that is not the end of the story. We discovered at the same time that we had saved enough to buy a new suit—the first item on my original list. Then an organization paid me for judging some music auditions. Their payment was the exact amount that Sears advertised for a washing machine. So we got the washer—part of want number two.

Late that fall, I went to teach about using music in other cultures at a missionary orientation center. While there, I was having lunch with a friend whose calling was to Africa. I asked him, "Norm, did you get your visa for Nigeria?" He replied that Nigeria was not then granting any visas for missionaries to enter the country. I asked, "Have they assigned you another country?" He told me that he and his family were going to Upper Volta (now Burkina Faso).

In my ignorance I asked where that was. He told me that it was inland and sub-Sahara. He added, "The missionaries wrote that it is so hot and dry that we should not bring our dryer, so now we need to get rid of it. You couldn't use a dryer, could you?" Almost in disbelief, I assured him that we needed a dryer desperately. Norman asked, "What kind of dryer connections do you have?" and I answered that they were electric. He then gave me the bad news that the connections on his dryer were gas.

The next morning, however, we were preparing to have a worship service. A missionary going to Brazil came in with a question for the group. "Wait, before we start, my wife and I have an emergency. We've been packing our crates for shipping, and we just received a letter telling us that our dryer connections are gas, but we have an electric dryer. Is there anyone here who would be willing to exchange a gas dryer for an electric dryer?" Now we had our dryer.

We had both the washer and the dryer. Standing in the utility room after the installation, I commented to Laverne, "This has such a surprising twist. We used to pray for things and often didn't get them. Now this fall I have found myself attending to other matters and not concerned about things. Yet we have all the first items on my original want list of last August—the new suit, the washer, and the dryer. Still, we haven't prayed for them. Why did we fail to get them when we prayed, but then got them when we didn't pray?" She asked me, "What is that verse that has meant so much to you this fall?" I answered, "Matthew 6:33, Seek first His kingdom and His righteousness." Laverne pursued it, "And what does the rest of the verse say?"

Of course the verse assures us, "And all these things shall be added to you." Suddenly, with a burst of insight, I told Laverne, "All my life I have been about the wrong business. I thought those 'things' in Matthew 6:33 were my business, and I've tried to attend to them. Now I find out that God's kingdom and righteousness are *my* business and *God's* business is my things. When I released my things to God and started attending to *my* business—which is God's kingdom and righteousness—I freed God to attend to *His* business, which is my things. I have released the hand of God to work in what He loves to work in—our things. Our things are *His* business."

As your first step in ridding yourself of the dominion of sin in your life, make a list of the wants or desires of your life. Then check one against the other to see if your various wants enhance and empower one another. Mark those desires that conflict with or neutralize your nobler desires. Ask the Lord to give you the greater obsession of always seeking His kingdom.

Conclusion

Christ's desires within me facilitate the work of the Father in my life. God's goal is Christ's integration of my mind in my life. The first step in attaining that integration is to change my wants. My growth in holy desires is attainable only by seeking the kingdom above anything else. Christ set an example for me by His simple desire to be about "His Father's business." He helps me in His office as Refiner and Purifier. He wants me to want what He wants.

Free Indeed

Let this mind be in you.

Wants can be good. Jesus wanted to honor His Father. But wants can also be bad, like some of mine. The *area* of wants is itself neutral; that is, wants can be good or bad. They can go in either direction. I was on the verge of discovering other areas of bondage that are also neutral. The area of habits, for example, is neither good nor bad, but neutral.

Other areas are damaging in themselves. For example, the area of hurts or grudges is destructive. Individual resentments are antagonistic to the mind of Christ, but the entire area of grudges is damaging. God wanted to deal first with the neutral areas of bondage (wants that are neither good or bad) before He dealt with the damaging areas (every one of which is bad).

Neutral Areas of Bondage

Habits

One afternoon Laverne was waiting for me to pick her up. I forgot the appointment. In those days I was absent-minded. I usually made the excuse that I was a professor. People expected me to have my mind on deeper matters. When I suddenly remembered the appointment, I realized that she had been waiting for me an hour, so I drove quickly across town to get her. I arrived with profuse apologies and begged her to forgive me. Of course, she granted forgiveness immediately but then said, "If you are serious about sin not being master over you, don't you think you ought to pray about your absent-mindedness? After all, does a bad habit honor the indwelling Spirit?"

That gave me pause for thought. A few days after that I was reading in Mark when the phrase, "According to His custom, He once more began to teach them" (10:1), caught my attention. Jesus had habits! He was in the habit of going to the synagogue on the Sabbath (Luke 4:16). Gethsemane must have been a favorite location, for He had the custom of going to the Mount of Olives when He was in Jerusalem (Luke 22:39). Prayer was one of His habits (Mark 1:35; Luke 6:12). All of His habits were good, and I knew that all of mine were not.

I realized that the Holy Spirit was showing me that freedom in the area of lusts or desires was only a beginning. Sin in other areas could bind me as well. The Lord clearly was demonstrating another area of bondage—my habits.

In my next quiet time, I took my pencil and paper and prayed for the Lord to reveal to me all my habits, healthy and unhealthy. I wrote them down and saw some habits He wanted to eradicate. Again, in my helplessness, I prayed for the Lord to show me how to eliminate all that was displeasing to Him. A bad habit (like absent-mindedness) reveals an area of our life that is not under the control of the Holy Spirit.

Most of my bad habits resulted from carelessness. I knew I could not make the changes by personal discipline. Rather I yielded more consciously to the constant rule of the Holy Spirit. My habits were changed from being careless to being Spirit-ruled.

The Lord had undertaken a new work in my life. I knew that He wanted me to grow in the mind of Christ, and He was repatterning my thought habits. In biblical language, He was transforming my mind. I had not expected Him to start by radically reforming my desires and freeing me in the areas of bondage. "Be ye transformed by the renewing of your mind" is a command (Rom. 12:2 KJV). Somehow I had not perceived transforming my mind as an active, continuing process. Nevertheless, that is what God wants: we are to "be renewed in the spirit of [our] mind" (Eph. 4:23 KJV). God had begun a process of transformation; I could only cooperate.

Loyalties

One day I found myself arguing with a friend over a certain matter, and as we talked I became defensive. At that point the Holy Spirit whispered that defensiveness was a sign of carnality. Here was another signal from God, so I responded. (Remember that being responsive is one of the qualities of a Christlike mind.) The conviction was strong enough that I prayed through the matter. The Lord was saying that I had been defending a false loyalty.

We usually think of loyalty as an admirable quality, one we try to cultivate in our children. Jesus Himself had loyalties. He was loyal to His Father. He loyally protected the disciples at the time of His arrest. But we are to be like Jesus in every respect, and now the Lord was bringing to light the fact that not all loyalties are Christlike. I had not realized that a loyalty could be false or superfluous.

I made a list of all my loyalties and then prayed through the items on the list. My list was too long. Loyalties, like wants, should be pure before the Lord. I discovered that I had never weighed my loyalties according to spiritual value. Some of them I eliminated as valueless, the others I assigned a new value according to their spiritual weight. I found that I could be loyal to anything I could pray for. Anything I could pray for, I could work for. The final result was an almost complete restructuring of my value system. God changed my loyalties from being scattered to being prayerful.

Relationships

The next area in which the Holy Spirit began working to free me from the bondage of sin was relationships. Relationships can be healthy, like Jesus' relationship to His mother (John 19:26–27) or to Mary, Martha, and Lazarus (Luke 10:38; John 11:5).

Yet our relationships may not be quite so healthy. The Spirit may see possessiveness of which we are not conscious. Deliberately, I "gave" my wife to the Lord by saying, "Lord, I ask You to make her love You more than she loves me." I asked God to make her priorities those of Mark 12:29–31—our love for God must be placed first, far above all earthly loves.

When I prayed that prayer about my daughter, I had to add, "And this means that if You want to take her to Africa or some other distant field, her love and service to You must outrank her love and service to us." (Incidentally, I have prayed this prayer about each of my grand-children as they came along.)

I found the Spirit leading me to make a list of all my relationships —my boss, my friends, my colleagues, and others—and to give them to the Lord to serve whatever purposes He had in bringing them into my life. Slowly, little by little, I came to realize that every relationship in my life was to be a relationship of service to God. God was transforming my thought patterns. My relationships had changed from serving self unconsciously to serving God consciously.

Prejudices

Next the Holy Spirit began working on my *prejudices*. I didn't think I had any. Under the leadership of the Spirit, I found deep, hidden prejudices. Naaman was angry when Elijah told him to bathe in the Jordan, and asked, "Are not Abanah and Pharpar, the rivers of Damascus, better than all the waters of Israel?" (2 Kings 5:12). The Pharisees were prejudiced; they asked Jesus' disciples, "Why is your Teacher eating with the tax-gatherers and sinners?" (Matt. 9:11). Yet Jesus was not, that is, He had no crippling prejudices. He chose Zaccheus as a follower (Luke 19:5). He ministered to a Samaritan woman when Jews normally despised Samaritans (Luke 4:7–26).

Parenthetically, we should note that Jesus was prejudiced about God's previous revelation. In Mark 7:8–13, Jesus censured the Pharisees for placing tradition above the Law of Moses. He told the cleansed leper to "present the offering that Moses commanded" (Matt. 8:4). He held the Law in high regard and said that He came to fulfill it (Matt. 5:17). Prejudices like the areas mentioned so far can be neutral. They can be good or bad.

In these times, dangerous prejudices for the believer are those of race or ethnic group. Prejudice imperils reconciliation, and God wants all His peoples to be reconciled. Prejudice is not the mind of Christ.

Under the supervision of God's Spirit, we may find other unsuspected prejudices. For example, some believers unconsciously think that if God works a certain way in their life, He will work that way with other believers. This is true in the area of spiritual gifts. We sometimes think that the use of our particular gift or gifts is the only way God can work in the lives of others. Some Christian workers think that all are called to their same calling. Men or women may think the other sex is failing when it does not see their perspective.

If we are prejudiced about the way God must work in anyone's life, we are limiting the sovereignty of God. If God is sovereign, there can be no prejudice on our part that would limit His working in our lives. Once again, I had to make a list, this time of prejudices. I had not suspected their lurking presence—"peccadilloes," as the world calls them—but they limit the control of God.

In each of the areas named so far, I had to make a list and pray fervently about the bondage inherent in false lusts, habits, loyalties, relationships, and prejudices. I prayed fervently over each list as a prelude to the deeper working of the Spirit in freeing me from the several areas of bondage.

Ambitions

Not surprisingly, the Lord next led me to the bondage inherent in my ambitions. These again were neutral. Jesus had the ambition to finish the work the Father sent Him to do (John 4:34).

Our ambitions, on the other hand, reveal sin in the area of pride. Being honest with the Lord is difficult in this area, so I had to pray that the Lord would help me be open to Him as I made the list of my ambitions. I had not consciously articulated certain ambitions; they were really an unconscious hope. In my prayers I became aware of ambitions I had never admitted to myself.

After I made the list, I tried sincerely to give these ambitions to the Lord. Again I freed Him to do anything He needed to do to accomplish His aim. Many of my ambitions would have brought honor to me, sometimes indirectly. Now the transformation began. The Spirit wanted me to eliminate many of my personal ambitions and to develop ambitions that would honor the Lord or advance His kingdom in some significant way.

Duties

The next area of bondage the Spirit directed me to was a real shock. He began to convict me that some of my duties were an obstacle to complete freedom. One of the works of the Spirit is to produce in us a sense of "ought to" about our basic Christian works. The conviction stole upon me that I was carrying on several busy activities for which I was not gifted or called. Under the close supervision of the Holy Spirit, I discovered a compulsiveness about the duties I was carrying out in my life.

I made a study of the times when Jesus said "I must"—I must be about My Father's business . . . I must preach in the other cities also, for thereunto was I sent . . . I must journey on to Jerusalem. A prophet cannot perish outside Jerusalem. Jesus' duties related to bringing God's kingdom. Indeed, God expects us to fulfill our duties. We are, for example, to be sure that our love for Him is the supreme love of our lives. We are to honor our parents and pay our tithes ("These things ought ye to have done . . .").

To have the mind of Christ, we must know what God wants us to do. Jesus knew what the Father wanted Him to do; "We must work the works of Him who sent Me" (John 9:4). But we also must know what we are not required to do. "One thing is needful" (Luke 10:42 KJV). I made my list of duties, and discovered through prayerful effort how many of them were not of God. Ridding myself of superfluous duties required an unexpected determination, but in the process I found myself thinking about the kingdom and my role in it.

Debt

Now the Lord began to speak to me about the bondage of debt. Monetary debt is serious. The Christian is not really free until he or she is out of debt. Getting out of debt may require discipline. It can also be perilous to become overly indebted for the favors people do us.

The continuing work of the Spirit introduced still another way of looking at debt. The Bible does not speak of Jesus having any debts, although He undoubtedly felt strong obligations to His disciples and the women who attended Him (John 17:12). Paul used "debt" to indicate the ministry he was called to: "I am debtor both to the Greeks, and to the Barbarians, both to the wise, and to the unwise" (Rom. 1:14 KJV). God had already narrowed my ministry. My sense of debt was transformed to apply to the ministry God had given me.

Possessions

Now it was time for the Lord to free me from my possessions. Most of us are bound, more than we know, by the things we own. Few Western Christians know the kind of life that Christ lived, owning nothing except His clothes.

The Lord began by requiring that I give Him our house. Laverne agreed with me that the Lord should dictate our use of the house, and we dedicated it to Him. He quickly sent a series of students, friends, "hippies" (street people, usually homeless people), and others for us to host, obviously as a test of the commitment we had made. Moreover, I had to disciple or teach these guests as best I could under the circumstances (this required that I give the Lord my time to use as He pleased).

The Lord seemed either to find unusual uses for our possessions or to dispossess us of them. Again, little by little, God transformed our mind-set from one of ownership to one of stewardship.

In all these transformations, we were being freed—freed from the world as we had known it, freed from inhibitions, freed from the necessity to "look" a certain way to our friends and the world, freed from time-worn but false conceptions of happiness and well-being, freed from the restraints of secret bonds we had not realized were there. Not only were we "freed from," we were "freed to" act—freed to let God have first place, freed to minister to His body, freed to move into new and deeper lessons on Christlikeness. Previously, outside forces dictated the structure of my thought life. Now I found the Holy Spirit directing my thoughts from within.

My thoughts were already being repatterned. Remember the evaluation of our lusts, ambitions, pride, and addictions in chapter 1? These were disappearing from my conscious thought life. I found my mind moving toward the right side of that evaluation in a significant number of areas.

Would you like for your thoughts to be repatterned also? Try making your own lists of your personal habits, loyalties (these may include institutions), relationships (these should be with persons), prejudices, ambitions, duties, debts, and possessions. And take your time. Remember that God works in process, and sometimes that is very slow. It took me fourteen months to make these lists I have described so far and to feel progress in these areas. Each time you make a list, you will probably discover some bondage to sin in that area. Tell God that He has the freedom to do anything He has to do to lead you to complete freedom.

Even Jesus had wants—He wanted to honor His Father. He had habits —prayer and synagogue attendance. He was prejudiced (or convinced) about God's previous revelation. His ambition was to complete the work assigned Him. His duties were focused on the kingdom of God. His debts were ministry related—what He was anointed to do (Luke 4:18). He possessed only the clothing on His back. His ministry was financed by a group of women.

Christ's mental orientation in these areas was perfect. As we have seen, mine was not. I had wrongful lusts, bad habits, superfluous loyalties, and so on. The areas we have covered so far could be neutral, spiritual or unspiritual.

Periodically, I continue to remake the lists, and each time I discover that the Lord is taking me deeper and deeper into His freedom. You may want to remake your lists from time to time. Making the lists and giving them to God facilitates the process of "perfecting holiness" (2 Cor. 7:1). The Lord's freedom is, after all, freedom from sin. In the process, God is transforming my mind. The mind of Christ cannot be unholy.

Damaging Areas of Bondage

By now the Lord had prepared me for a step I could not have taken the year before. The Holy Spirit was about to lead me to recognize areas of bondage foreign to the mind of Christ. He had taken me through the neutral areas of bondage in order to help me deal with three areas that were not neutral, but damaging. Habits, loyalties, and even ambitions need not be harmful. Now the Lord introduced into my consciousness areas that were themselves destructive. Christ had no fears, weaknesses, or grudges; they are alien to His mind. Those entire areas must become foreign to our minds. The probing was going deeper and requiring more.

Fears

The first of these damaging areas was my fear. I wrote down all the fears I could think of and saw that most of them grew out of self-protectiveness. Even though I had given my debts and possessions to the Lord, some of my fears had to do with money or the lack of it. I had certain fears about my family. Some of them revolved around job security, but in all of them I discovered the element of self-protectiveness. Basically, my fears revealed a lack of trust in God, so I had to pray much about the depth of my faith. To have the mind of Christ is to trust in the Father's provision. Only He can protect us; only He can protect our families.

After I wrote down all the fears I could think of, I gave them to the Lord. I asked Him to transform my mind in whatever direction He wished. He began to develop in me a unique security—the security of resting in Christ's finished work in me and for me. I was being changed from a stance of self-protectiveness to a stance of security.

Weaknesses

The next area of damaging bondage was in the area of my weaknesses. We excuse our weaknesses by saying that we were born with them or our environment caused them. For example, one of my weaknesses was that

I could not speak effectively in public (like Moses), although the particular witness God was giving me then demanded that I do that. I am basically a shy person, although I had developed various techniques to mask my shyness. I had found the means to compensate for other weaknesses and tried to hide them from others.

The truth was that I had never really talked to the Lord about my weaknesses. So I made the usual list and prayed carefully about it. I asked the Lord to strengthen me where necessary and to use my weak points somehow for His glory. In this way, God transformed my weaknesses from being a tool of Satan to being a tool for His use.

Hurts

The Holy Spirit had one area of bondage yet to deal with—my hurts or grudges. In retrospect, I am grateful that the Spirit saved these for last. We have to dig past our subconscious and unconscious mind to be sure of these. We want the Lord to be thorough in dealing with us, and that is His intention.

I made my list, and there were many of these. As one example, in 1959, while I was working on my Ph.D., I experienced revival in my personal life. Before the renewal, I had been successful in musicology and had achieved a reputation for knowledge and sophistication in that field. After the renewal, I found myself with a new set of values. The reputation I had so eagerly sought was now hollow.

My new values required a witness for Christ that began to change my reputation. From being a witness for the world and its values, I was becoming a witness for Christ, and that was not fashionable on the campus of North Texas State University in 1959. Fellow students who had looked up to me now looked down on me, and on occasion I found myself the target of their jokes.

One of the men who became haughty about the change in my life was a Christian. After we finished our doctoral work, I occasionally saw him at professional meetings, and he always cleverly worked into the conversation that I was a religious fanatic. Had I been quick-witted enough, I could have used his remarks as an occasion for a sharp witness, but I was too shy and reticent to argue. So I bottled it up and resented him.

I had others. One man had lied to try to worm his way into a position I was occupying. Others had taken advantage of me. The depth of my bottled-up resentments dismayed me. But the Lord had been preparing me through the previous year to deal with these grudges. I finished the list, prayed over each of them, and asked the Lord to forgive me for the undue rancor I felt in some cases and to forgive my offenders for the wrongs they had done out of selfishness.

Later that morning I was praying as I walked to the school where I taught. I asked the Lord, "How well do I really understand forgiveness?" I remembered Matthew 5:43–44: "You have heard that it was said, 'You shall love your neighbor, and hate your enemy.' But I say to you, love your enemies, and pray for those who persecute you." Now what could I legitimately pray for the fellow who made fun of my relationship to Christ? I told the Lord, "I must ask for something he would understand, and the only thing he understands is money!" I groped for an understanding of the Christlike thing to ask for him, but repeatedly was brought back to the subject of money—a kind of god to my friend.

Unexpectedly it occurred to me that I have various degrees, certificates, and awards that I could hang on the wall if I wanted to (I don't). Yet for the changes of the previous year—my new freedom from the many areas of bondage—I had no certificates, no outer or visible proof that the changes that had taken place in my thought processes were of real spiritual value. Although I thought they were of God, I had no tangible evidence that they really were. I wholeheartedly wanted to pray spiritually and intelligently (1 Cor. 14:15), but I needed a signal from God that I was on the right track.

So I prayed, "Lord, I pray that You will speak to Bill about Yourself through money. I ask that You cause an unexpected windfall suddenly to fall in his lap so miraculously that he will know that You are indeed working in his life and that You care for him—and then, Lord, make him call me about what happened. If he calls me, I won't need a certificate. I will know that You are indeed signaling me and that You really want me free from these resentments and from all the other areas of bondage."

Almost immediately, Bill called. He said, "T.W., you can't imagine what has happened." And then he told me about an unexpected windfall that was so miraculous that he knew God had done it. I told him, "Bill, you can't imagine how much this means to me." At first he didn't believe me, but my sincerity ultimately came through and we became fast friends. As we talked, I realized that God had worked through my resentment and subsequent change to perform a miracle in Bill's life. Then the Lord directed me to another transformation: He had transformed my resentment into love.

Once you have begun to feel freedom in the neutral areas, you can proceed to make the lists of these more difficult, damaging areas. The neutral areas are comparatively easy; the damaging areas require concentration and much prayer. If you do the neutral areas first, you will discover the encouragement of seeing God work and will enter the last three areas with more confidence.

After you make the lists, once again give God the liberty to do anything He needs to do to give you complete freedom. The Holy Spirit may direct you to areas I have not named. He may work your transformation in a completely different direction from the one He took me through. He is free, too.

Anyone can be free in the areas I have described. God's intention is that we be free from this world's mind-set. In doing that, God binds us to His mind-set, the mind of Christ. It must be one or the other. When we think like God thinks, we are free from the bonds of Satan.

Jesus Christ was the freest human being who ever walked on earth. As His ministry moved into various phases, He had to make decisions—ministry decisions, decisions about what to say and when to say it, where to go and when to go, always watching the timing of His Father. He spoke often of "His hour." His decisions were always perfect. He began the extensive Galilean ministry only after an initial, brief ministry in Jerusalem. He terminated the Galilean ministry to devote attention to the training of His twelve disciples. He embarked on the final trip to Jerusalem at the right time. He raised Lazarus at a time when He knew that it would provoke the final jealous decision of the Sanhedrin to execute Him. *Only in freedom can we make spiritual decisions.* Jesus' life is a monument of freedom.

Why is our freedom from the bondage of sin so important to having the mind of Christ? The person with the mind of Christ has focused attention. When we are in bondage, our attention is on our own lusts, fixations, loyalties, ambitions, grudges, and all that binds us to the world system. Christ's freedom within us facilitates the mental quality of attention—attention to God, to His word, to prayer, and to His voice. God's goal is our freedom.

That freedom has no earthly measures. Our danger is that we will think, *I'm not as sinful as so-and-so.* The only measure of our freedom is the Lord Jesus Christ Himself. Our growth in freedom from sin can only be measured by Christ's sinlessness.

The subject here is not imputed righteousness. God's imputation of Christ in us is a matter of faith and is important, but this is a different subject. I am talking now about the outworking of our faith. Fruitful faith is practical, and we are responsible for that outworking. Christ wants us to be as free as He is.

Conclusion

Christ's freedom within me facilitates the mental quality of attention. God's goal is my complete freedom from any bondage to this world system. I can measure my growth in freedom from sin only by Christ's sinlessness. He gives freedom in His office as Deliverer. He set me free.

chapter four

The Lifestyle of Christ

Which was also in Christ Jesus

O ne Friday morning I was praising the Lord for the new purity in my life, the freedom from sin I was now experiencing. The satanic opposite of purity, lust, had given way to real freedom. As I reflected on what had happened to me, I became conscious of the obscene speech of one of my friends. He habitually brought in innuendos that came from a mind apparently obsessed with sex. So I prayed that God would purify him.

Then I thought of a lady who seemed to cultivate friendships for what they could do for her. That was a different kind of impurity—impurity of motive. I prayed for her purity. The longer I thought about it, it appeared to me that most of my friends were impure in one way or another, so I set out to pray for them.

As I was doing that, I sensed that I was somehow wrong in my praying. The Holy Spirit shocked me when He convicted me that I had perverted the quality of purity and was now puritanical.[1]

Each virtue has satanic opposites. Each virtue also has satanic perversions that are much more subtle and easy to slip into unawares. This, of course, is not the mind of Christ. It disappointed me that I had gone so wrong while trying to develop a biblical quality. I prayed about my mistake and asked God to show me what led me into the error.

Without question the Pharisees knew much more about their Bible (the Torah) than I did about mine, and yet they were puritanical. The

Pharisees (and I) had made two basic mistakes. We cannot measure our purity by ourselves, and we cannot measure it by comparing ourselves to others.

Only the Lifestyle of Christ Defines the Virtues

The Bible tells us to "consider Jesus, the Apostle and High Priest of our confession" (Heb. 3:1). It is not enough to know what the Bible says about purity; we also must know how Jesus lived out the virtue. He came to show us what the Creator really had in mind when He made us. He became like us (Heb. 2:14, 17) so that we could become like Him (Rom. 8:29). We must define the virtues in reference to the life and personality of Jesus. The Bible tells us to "fix our eyes" on Him (Heb. 12:2). On the basis of what the Bible records, we must discern how He expresses His righteousness.

Pure

Jesus was pure but never talked about it. No man ever lived who had more adoring women around him than Jesus. They supported Him with their means (Luke 8:3), remained at the cross longer than others, and were first at the tomb. If He had been lustful, He could have taken advantage of this adoration.

Yet Peter, who was in Jesus' inmost circle and watched Him closely for three and a half years, described Him as a "lamb unblemished and spotless" (1 Pet. 1:19). John, another of the inner circle, said, "in Him there is no sin" (1 John 3:5). Matthew, one of the intimate twelve, was the one who recorded His words on purity of heart (Matt. 5:8). Those who knew Him best recorded a mental self-command unique among humans.

He was not lustful, but neither was He puritanical. Puritanical people are narrow in their selection of friends. Jesus befriended so many tax collectors, prostitutes, and down-and-outs that they called Him a "friend of sinners." His broadness was inclusive; He readily accepted invitations to eat with self-righteous Pharisees and with "sinful" tax collectors. The witness of His friends was that He never yielded to lust or to any other impurity, yet He also never perverted purity. He was simply and completely *pure.*

I was to learn that Christians can pervert each virtue. Each new step introduced me to new dimensions of the wisdom of God.

Peaceable

Jesus was the wisdom of God (1 Cor. 1:24). Therefore He was all that James 3:17 says that wisdom is. The first quality of wisdom in that verse is purity. The second quality named is peaceable. We will look at the satanic opposite of each quality and at their perversions.

The opposite of *peaceable* is *fussy*. Jesus was peaceable. He discouraged competition. Three times the disciples got into a fuss about which of them was the greatest, but Jesus told them, "Whoever wishes to be first among you shall be your slave." He told them that He Himself "did not come to be served, but to serve, and to give His life a ransom for many" (Matt. 20:28).

Yet we can pervert peace. One of the perversions of peace is compromise. Jesus cautioned, "Do not think that I came to bring peace on the earth; I did not come to bring peace, but a sword. For I came to set a man against his father, and a daughter against her mother, and a daughter-in-law against her mother-in-law; and a man's enemies will be the members of his household" (Matt. 10:34–36). In all His tranquility, He drew hard lines and did not hesitate to express them in Matthew 23. We must not prostitute or distort His qualities or His ideas. Wisdom can discern the difference in the virtue and the perversion. We need wisdom.

Gentle

The Greek word for *gentle* in James 3:17 denotes gentleness in action. The opposite is *harsh*. Jesus showed biblical gentleness in His dealings with Peter. He could benevolently beckon Peter to walk on water only to reprimand Peter's little faith moments later (Matt. 14:28–32). He could lavishly call Peter "blessed" for his insight and then rebuke him for refusing to embrace God's plan for Jesus (Matt. 16:17, 23).

You can understand this gentleness if you think of a good dentist (this is how I choose my dentist—on the basis of this Christlike quality). Suppose my dentist refused to tell me about a cavity so he wouldn't have to hurt me by giving me a shot of Novocaine. He might be a good friend, but would he be a good dentist? He would be perverting gentleness. The perversion of gentleness is an unkind restraint. A good parent, a good dentist, or a functioning Christian must be gentle without perversion. Jesus' dealings with Peter show a restraint that never became unkind. The gentleness we seek is the application of the consummate skill of Christ to the removal of imperfections in Christ's body.

Entreatable

James adds entreatable as a quality of wisdom. An entreatable person is glad to serve. He or she does not object to someone asking them a favor. The opposite of this virtue is being unapproachable. Some people retreat from every opportunity to serve.

The perversion is to be a yes-man. Jesus was approachable, but He was not obsequious. He knew the difference. We need His discernment to know that difference. Not once did He ever turn down a request for healing, although He tested the faith of the Syro-Phoenician woman (Matt. 15:21–28) and delayed going to Lazarus so that He might perform a greater miracle (John 11:4). When others were rebuking Bartimaeus, Jesus heard him (Mark 10:48–49). Jesus' story is one of constant availability, but He was not fawning or servile.

Merciful

The next quality in God's wisdom is merciful. The opposite of *merciful* is *merciless*—an un-Christlike adjective to apply to a believer. The perversion is to be indulgent. We also find indulgence frequently within the body of Christ.

We often equate mercy with compassion. Jesus' repeated healings reveal a profound sympathy for the hurt, the impaired, and the suffering. At times, He determined to heal in spite of official opposition (Mark 3:1–5). Matthew, especially, often mentions the compassion that a large crowd aroused in Jesus (9:36, 14:14, 15:32). I believe the tears at Lazarus's tomb were partially a result of the empathy He felt for Mary and Martha. Through Jesus we know the compassionate heart of God, yet never marred by indulgence.

Fruitful

James 3:17 tells us that God's wisdom is fruitful. The term can apply to the fruit of the Spirit or to the fruit of our witness for Christ. The opposite is fruitless and that is a danger. Jesus was the most fruitful man who ever lived. He had the fruit of the Spirit, and He drew thousands of people to Himself. He changed the course of world history. His followers (His "fruit") number in the millions.

The perversion is to be obsessed with numbers. God blesses some few persons with an all-consuming desire to win souls for Christ, and these become fruitful people. The obsession, as an obsession, is relatively rare. It occurs only in persons preoccupied with numbers at the expense of genuine conversion. For the sake of effective witness, we avoid that perversion.

Steadfast

After fruitfulness in the James verse on wisdom comes "without wavering," or steadfast. The opposite is wavering. Christ always remained unwavering in His life purpose. Once He set His face toward the cross, nothing—not the pleas of a beloved disciple nor the dread of the process—could deter Him from carrying out the divine intention.

The perversion is to be inflexible or rigid. Christ was not that either. Entreatable persons are flexible. If we are steadfast *and* entreatable, people can interrupt us. For example, Jesus accepted Simon's intrusion on His prayer time (Mark 1:35–37). He interrupted a trip to heal a little girl who was dying, to deal with the woman with an issue of blood (Mark 5:21–43). Jesus was steadfast but had the discernment not to be inflexible.

Honest

The final quality of wisdom in James 3:17 is "without hypocrisy," or honest. No one can attribute any lie or play acting to Christ. He is truth (John 14:6). Jesus insisted on inner perfection and confronted the hypocrisy of the Pharisees with terrifying honesty (Luke 11:37–52).

The perversion of honesty is being brutal. Christ was not that. In His dealings with the Pharisees, He was not malicious. He simply spoke the truth in all its fearfulness. Only discernment knows how to integrate honesty, integrity, and confrontation, and Christ Himself was wisdom.

The Lifestyle of Christ Defines the Fruit of the Spirit

To have the mind of Christ is to have the wisdom of God or the qualities of James 3:17. We must also have the fruit of the Spirit, for that too is the mind of Christ. Just as the qualities of wisdom can be perverted or have an opposite, so can the fruit of the Spirit.

Jesus lived His life consummately in the spiritual realm. Jesus was "led up by the Spirit" (Matt. 4:1) and was "full of the Holy Spirit" (Luke 4:1) as He approached the temptation experience. After the temptation, "Jesus returned to Galilee in the power of the Spirit" (Luke 4:14). To begin His Galilean ministry, He announced, "The Spirit of the Lord is upon Me" (Luke 4:18). He said, "I cast out demons by the Spirit of God" (Matt. 12:28). The mind of Christ is controlled by the Spirit and will demonstrate the fruit of the Spirit (Gal. 5:22–23).

Love

The fruit of the Spirit begins with love. One opposite is hate, but we can discover many opposites—fear, aversion, animosity, or hostility. Christ's life never showed hostility.

Jesus loved. That was His life. "Having loved His own who were in the world, He loved them to the end" (John 13:1). Jesus described the action of perfect love—"Greater love has no one than this, that one lay down his life for his friends" (John 15:13)—and then proceeded to do that in the cross, the highest expression of love of all time.

We can pervert love into permissiveness, protectiveness, and possessiveness. Jesus was none of these. He would not allow His disciples to stop short of His high standards. Jesus did not choose them for their quickness of discernment, for they often missed His purposes. For example, James and John wanted to call fire down from heaven to destroy the Samaritan village (Luke 9:54). Jesus constantly corrected the disciples' erroneous impressions, but always in love. He loved but did not pervert love; He was discriminating.

Joy

The second fruit of the Spirit is joy. The opposite is *hurt*. We need not harbor resentment when people mistreat us.

Joy is higher than pleasure. We seek pleasure, but joy is a fruit. Joy characterized the life of Jesus. At times Jesus knew joy derived from the occasion (the return of the seventy in Luke 10:21). He enjoyed the fellowship of the Bethany home (Luke 10:38–29; John 11:3, 5). Still, His highest joy was a continuum that depended not on circumstances but on the deepest level of His being.

He had been speaking of His obedience to His Father when He told the disciples, "These things I have spoken to you, that My joy may be in you, and that your joy may be made full" (John 15:11). Later in the same discourse, He promised that their joy after His resurrection would be indestructible, a permanent feature in their lives (John 16:22). This discourse is commonly called the Last Discourse, spoken on the night before He died. From this speech, He went to the cross. Facing that hideous punishment, He retained His joy.

Two perversions of joy are a preoccupation with gratification and frenzy. (Each virtue may have several opposites and several perversions.) All of Jesus' activity was deliberate. The Gospels record no moment of self-gratification. Joy also is not a mania but a continuing and untouchable delight in the Lord.

Peace

God's Spirit also produces peace. The James 3:17 "peaceable" describes an outer way of acting; this quality in Galatians 5:22 is an inner peace. Jesus could bequeath His kind of peace to His disciples. Significantly, this bequest only comes at the end of His life, after they had observed Him over a long time. He told them, "These things I have spoken to you, that in Me you may have peace. In the world you have tribulation, but take courage; I have overcome the world" (John 16:33).

The opposite is war. In chapter 2 we saw that sin can produce inner war in us. The perversion is being neutral. Jesus warned against lukewarmness. He baptized "with the Holy Spirit and fire" (Matt. 3:11). What is wrong with being lukewarm? When you are lukewarm, you are trying to be hot and cold at the same time; you are aiming at opposite qualities. Jesus said He would vomit out the lukewarm.

Long-suffering

The next virtue in the Galatians verse is long-suffering—an old English word, but more picturesque than *patient*. Jesus suffered long with His disciples. He often had to reteach material He had already covered. Repeatedly the Lord chided the disciples for their "little faith" (Matt. 8:26, 14:31, 16:8; Mark 4:40). The disciples heard Him repeatedly say that the faith of those healed was the effective force in some of His miracles (Matt. 9:29; Luke 7:50). They heard Him commend the faith of the centurion (Matt. 8:10) and of the Syro-Phoenician woman (Matt. 15:28).

In spite of their slowness to learn, He never gave up. On the final trip to Jerusalem, He again taught the disciples on faith (Luke 17:6). Even in the last week of His life, He was still working to convey to them the importance and the nature of faith (Matt. 21:18–22). He was long-suffering.

The opposite is impatience, and we have seen that Christ bore with the disciples' difficulties in understanding. The perversion is lenience. Jesus was not lenient, for He persisted year after year in His reteaching. That reiteration left a strong impression on His disciples.

Gentleness

Galatians adds the fruit of the Spirit of gentleness, or in some transla-
tions, *kindness*. This word (a different Greek word from the word for
gentle in James) describes disposition more than action.

Jesus dealt tenderly with children, with the helpless, with the lame
and impaired, and with His own disciples. After the Sermon on the Mount,
the leper pleaded, "Lord, if You are willing, You can make me clean."
Jesus' answer was gracious: "I am willing; be cleansed" (Matt. 8:2, 3).

Since this gentleness deals with disposition, the opposite is to be
hard. Jesus warned the Pharisees that Moses permitted divorce "because
of your hardness of heart" (Matt. 19:8). The perversion is to be soft.
Jesus was not soft when He pronounced the woes on the Pharisees and
teachers of the law in the temple (Matt. 23:13–36). With those that
needed firmness, Jesus was uncompromising. With the vulnerable, He
dealt sympathetically.

Goodness

Goodness is an important fruit of the Spirit. As Jesus used the word,
good always indicated that something or someone was functioning. Of
the two servants who invested well, the master said, "Well done, good
and faithful slave" (Matt. 25:21, 23). These servants functioned; they
produced. He said that a good tree would produce good fruit (Matt. 7:17);
that is, the tree functions properly according to God's design.

Jesus produced. No failure mars His record. After the healing of the
deaf man in the Decapolis, "They were utterly astonished, saying, 'He
has done all things well; He makes even the deaf to hear, and the dumb
to speak'" (Mark 7:37). Of His own works, He claimed, "The works
which the Father has given Me to accomplish, the very works that I do,
bear witness of Me, that the Father has sent Me. And the Father who sent
Me, He has borne witness of Me" (John 5:36–37). He was good. He
functioned.

The opposite of goodness is badness, or failure to function. In the
parable of the talents, one fellow did not function. He was worthless and
was cast "into the outer darkness" (Matt. 25:30).

The perversion (or one of them) is to be finicky nice. Jesus was far
more than merely nice, and He certainly was not fastidious or overly
meticulous. Jesus was the most wholesome man who ever lived. He
loved His friends and cultivated their companionship. He even loved to
eat. Every Pharisaic charge held some grain of truth. They called Him a

glutton (Matt. 11:19), so obviously they had noticed that He enjoyed eating. Some of them invited Him for meals. Jesus was no more a glutton than He was a drunkard, but He evidently ate with relish. He also knew when the next bite would be sin.

To Him, human life was good and worthy of His blessing. Jesus blessed the wedding at Cana. He truly was a human being, and He was wholesome. The mind of Christ is to enjoy the gifts of God, and to produce in the process.

Faithfulness

The seventh fruit of the Spirit is faith, or more accurately, faithfulness. Jesus is faithful in those things He has promised: "If you ask Me anything in My name, I will do it" (John 14:14); "I will not leave you as orphans; I will come to you" (John 14:18); "because I live, you shall live also" (John 14:19). He is faithful as our high priest: "He was faithful to Him who appointed Him" (Heb. 3:2). John calls Him the "faithful witness" in the salutation of his apocalyptic letter (Rev. 1:5). "Jesus Christ is the same yesterday and today, yes and forever" (Heb. 13:8). He is the goal by which we measure ourselves.

The opposite is faithlessness or fickleness. Fickle friends, fickle pastors, and fickle laymen plague the body of Christ. Jesus Christ, however, is dependable.

One perversion of faithfulness is stubbornness. Another is legalism. The Pharisees were legalistic. Jesus came to unmask and destroy that. Because Jesus revealed their error, we need not fall into it. They amplified the Mosaic Law into perversion. Obedience is a matter not of law but of the spirit. Faithfulness is a fruit of the Spirit.

Meekness

A neglected fruit of the Spirit is meekness. I prefer to use the term *meekness* to avoid confusing it with *gentleness*. True meekness is a humility coupled with strength. The word indicates a mildness, but that mildness would have no meaning if it were not administered by strength. Jesus was humble enough to choose the rough, rural districts of Galilee with its peasants. He was strong enough to confront hypocrisy. Yet He described Himself as "meek" (Matt. 11:29 KJV).

The opposite is arrogance. We have already seen that Christ was not arrogant, but lowly. When Miriam and Aaron became arrogant toward Moses, God corrected them. Moses was more humble "than any man who was on the face of the earth" (Num. 12:3). The perversion is weakness, and Jesus is clearly not weak. His address to the Pharisees and scribes in Matthew 23:2–36 is one of the strongest attacks in the Bible on those who oppose God. Jesus is the most powerful character in the Bible.

Temperance

A strong virtue follows next in Paul's inventory of spiritual fruit—temperance. Again the translation is difficult. The Greek renders this by a compound that refers to an inner strengthening. The translation *self-control* captures some of the idea. Temperance is also a discipline. We cannot impose it from without. The Spirit develops it within us. It grows like fruit grows.

The opposite is to be undisciplined, referring to a lack of self-control. Another opposite is self-indulgent. The perversion is fleshly effort or self-effort. Temperance is a fruit, and fruit is a natural result of the sap flowing from a trunk into a healthy branch.

Temperance is observable in such disciplines as prayer, Bible study, and witness. In Jesus, we see it in His night of prayer before choosing the disciples (Luke 6:12) or in His rising early to pray (Mark 1:35). His discipline also is obvious in the vast knowledge He had of the Old Testament. In Jesus, self-control was a fruit because of His intimate acquaintance with and dependence on the Holy Spirit.

The Christlike Life

In the chart below, you can see the Christly expression of each virtue contrasted with its opposites and perversions:

Christlike Virtues—James 3:17

Virtue	Opposite	Perversion
pure	impure	puritanical
peaceable	fussy	compromise
gentle	harsh	unkind restraint
entreatable	unapproachable	yes-man
merciful	merciless	indulgent
fruitful	fruitless	obsessed with numbers
steadfast	wavering	inflexible, rigid
honest	dishonest	brutal

Christlike Virtues—Galatians 5:22–23

Virtue	Opposite	Perversion
love	hate	possessiveness
joy	pain	frenzy
peace	war	neutrality
longsuffering	impatience	lenience
gentleness	hardness	softness
goodness	badness	finicky nice
faithfulness	faithlessness	legalism
meekness	arrogance	weakness
temperance	undisciplined	fleshly effort

One man, after he listened to the explanation of the chart above, exclaimed, "I just found out I'm the perfectly balanced Christian. I'm exactly half in the middle and half on the right!" That really is the problem with most of us. We want to be like the left, but often end up on the right.

After a friend of mine heard me teach on these opposites and perversions, he was struggling to apply these lessons to his life. In that process, he was able to share them in a meaningful way with his mother-in-law, who is a deeply spiritual Christian. He wrote:

> Yesterday I called my mother-in-law. She asked me if I had a few minutes and she shared with me something that happened at her church. It was a [negative] reaction she had to a particular person. She has a close walk with the Lord and has ministered to me countless times through the years.
>
> She said, "I thought I had won that battle of my inner struggle with this person years ago, and now here I am, in it again." I said, "This reminds me of something T. W. Hunt taught in 'The Mind of Christ.' I shared with her an example of the teaching from James 3:17 on the Christly mind and how it can become perverted. She said, "Oh, John, those insights are so convicting. What else is there?"
>
> I got out the syllabus and shared the whole chart with her. She told me, "This is why you called. The Lord wanted me to have that at this particular time. It will take me a while to digest it all, but I can see how I have missed the mind of

Christ." She called me later in the day and said, "Well, I have not stopped bleeding yet, but I would like to get a complete copy of the syllabus."

These lessons are for immediate application. Through prayer and the Holy Spirit, we *can* learn to discern the Christly. Satan tempts us in the middle of the chart, but he wants the world to look at Christians as though they were on the right side of the chart. Return to the chart now and go down the lists item by item. Ask God to show you whether you are on the left, in the middle, or on the right side of the chart. Then pray about those qualities in which you are not like Christ. Remember, it is God Himself who is the active agent (Phil. 2:13). He can change you if you ask Him to.

Conclusion

Christ's lifestyle in me springs from the mental quality of discernment. God's goal is that I have the wisdom of Christ and the fruit of the Spirit. I must not measure my wisdom and fruit by any other measure than Christ Himself. He enables me to have His qualities in His office as my Model. I look only to Him.

PART TWO

To Be Like Christ

chapter five

Jesus Christ, God's Son, Savior

*Who, being in the form of God,
thought it not robbery to be equal with God*

I had to apply the divinity of Christ in my life before I fully understood it. During the midfifties I made my career into my god. For about three years I served the false god of career in a fierce ambition to succeed. During those years I was active in church. None of my friends suspected that I was more devoted to me than to God.

The Lord must have a sense of humor. He chose to use my love of languages to speak to me. In the fall of 1959 one of my students gave me a little German New Testament. My immediate reaction was, "Oh, good, a chance to practice my German," not, "Oh, good, a Bible." I set it on a shelf so it would be handy when I found the chance to read it.

A few days later I was facing a lecture that would be a major chance to advance my career. I was excited at the professional opportunity it afforded, so the night before the lecture I set my alarm for 5:00 A.M. to give me one last chance to polish the speech. The next morning I got up, drank my coffee, and the lecture fell in place so smoothly that I was satisfied with it by 5:30. But now I was wide awake. I didn't want to wake anyone up, so I looked around for something to do until daylight. My eye caught the German Bible. Sitting on that couch was the best mistake I ever made.

I opened the Bible to the first chapter of John and began reading casually. The reading didn't remain casual for long, because the words said, "In the beginning was the word, and the word was with God, *and the word was God*" (emphasis added). I had not given serious thought to Christ's divinity for a long time. I didn't understand the shiver of excitement that seized my entire being with those words.

I read on and verse 4 stopped me short again: "In him was life." I knew that I could not say that. My life was dependent on air, water, and food. I must have an environment. Divinity requires nothing for its continuation. When I read verse 14, it was as though I had never read it before. It tells us that the divine Word was made incarnate and demonstrated God's glory.

All day long those verses haunted me. Somehow the brilliance and sophistication of my colleagues did not sound quite as glittery as I had imagined. That night I set my clock again for 5:00 A.M., but this time to read chapter 2 the next morning. Day after day as I progressed through John's Gospel I was overwhelmed with the cosmic grandeur of Christ. He is God and demonstrated divine authority repeatedly in those days in Jerusalem.

When I finished the Gospel, I decided to read the entire Bible through in a modern English translation. The day finally came when I read Exodus 3. In this chapter Moses is on the side of Mount Horeb (Sinai) and sees the burning bush. I cannot explain how God manipulates our consciousness, but that morning I knew that the burning bush was for me. And the words of God were also for me that morning: "Take your shoes off, for you are standing on holy ground."

I removed my shoes quickly and I knelt (you would have knelt, too). I have tried for many years to describe my mental state that morning and have never felt that I could easily express what I went through. I realized that I had faced the divinity of Christ, and yet my career was still my god. I felt judged. Somehow I also knew that the holiness of God was glorious and that I had chosen second best. It was much like going through judgment, and it was terrifying. On my knees I knew that God had confronted me through His word and that now I had to decide, once and for all, who would be sovereign in my life. I faced the fact that I had actually served myself; I was my own boss.

If Christ is indeed God and if He died for our sins (I had submerged myself in these facts in the Gospel of John), He deserves our allegiance and submission to His lordship. If He is God, He is boss. With all my heart I cried out to Christ, "From now on, You are Lord." And I meant that. His lordship eventually required a radical readjustment of my entire life. But I have never regretted my decision.

Six Attributes of Deity

The line above from the Philippian hymn claims that Jesus was "in the form of God." The New American Standard translation says that "He existed in the form of God." The King James Versions says that He "thought it not robbery to be equal with God." Since He is indeed God, He is equal with the Father and the Holy Spirit. He will share with them the unique attributes of divinity.

First, Jesus is *omnipotent.* Paul described His might as "the power that He has even to subject all things to Himself" (Phil. 3:21). The writer of Hebrews tells us that "He . . . upholds all things by the word of His power" (Heb. 1:3). Peter attributed to Him "the glory and dominion [Greek, *kratos,* "might"] forever and ever" (1 Pet. 4:11). He has absolute power. The people of His day came to Him in the conviction that He was all-powerful. The afflicted expected Him to have power and to use it. And we can expect Him to use His power on our behalf today.

Jesus is *omniscient.* When the Pharisees thought He drove out demons by Beelzebub, Jesus responded to them "knowing their thoughts" (Matt. 12:25). He would not entrust Himself to the superficial belief of the Jews, "because He did not need anyone to bear witness concerning man for He Himself knew what was in man" (John 2:25). When He told His disciples He had come from the Father and was returning to the Father, they confessed, "Now we know that You know all things" (John 16:30). They regarded His omniscience as being favorable to them. We need not be frightened that He knows our thoughts. His knowledge of us is coupled with His love and care for us.

To John on Patmos, Jesus declared, "I am He who searches the minds and hearts" (Rev. 2:23). Because we are to have the mind of Christ, we will have His help as He searches our mind and heart. The all-knowing One wants us to have His mind and heart.

Jesus, as God, is *omnipresent.* He promised His followers, "I am with you always" (Matt. 28:20). This is a promise that only all-presence can make. It was intended as reassurance and the early disciples accepted it as that. Christ's presence is to be enjoyed.

Jesus is *immortal.* Christians will live forever, that is, they have everlasting life, a life continuing after death into eternity. They do not have preexistence (existence before the creation of the universe), as immortality has. Micah's prophecy of the Messiah said, "But as for you, Bethlehem Ephrathah . . . From you One will go forth for Me to be ruler in Israel. His goings forth are from long ago, From the days of eternity" (Mic. 5:2).

In His transcendent intercessory prayer, Jesus prayed, "And now, glorify Thou Me together with Thyself, Father, with the glory which I had with Thee before the world was" (John 17:5). Later in the same prayer He prayed, "Thou didst love Me before the foundation of the world" (John 17:24). God had preexistence, and Jesus had preexistence.

Immortality continues forever. Jesus said, "I am the first and the last, and the living One; and I was dead, and behold, I am alive forevermore" (Rev. 1:17–18). At the end of the Bible, He says, "I am the Alpha and the Omega, the first and the last, the beginning and the end" (Rev. 22:13). This assures us that Christ will finish the work He has started in our lives.

With the other persons of the Trinity, Jesus shares *immutability,* that is, He will never change. His purpose does not vary: "He always lives to make intercession for them" (Heb. 7:25). His word will never change. Jesus claimed, "Heaven and earth will pass away, but My words shall not pass away" (Matt. 24:35). The Bible expressly says that He is immutable: "Jesus Christ is the same yesterday and today, yes and forever" (Heb. 13:8). We can be grateful that He is immutable. It means that He is dependable and that we can count on Him.

Jesus was and is *sinless.* Jesus asked the Jews, "Which one of you convicts Me of sin?" (John 8:46). The Bible tells us that Jesus "has been tempted in all things as we are," and adds that He was "yet without sin" (Heb. 4:15). John flatly says, "In Him there is no sin" (1 John 3:5). Only God is without sin.

Again this counts for us because the only righteousness we have is His (Jer. 23:6). He is made to be our own "righteousness and sanctification, and redemption" (1 Cor. 1:30). Theologians calls this "imputed" righteousness. That means that God looks at us as if we had the righteousness of Christ. He reads into us the righteousness of Christ.

Such imputed righteousness should discourage us from deliberate sin. We must not willfully make choices that violate the growing character of Christ in us. That is not His mind.

Our imputed righteousness is why 1 Corinthians 2:16 says that we have the mind of Christ. When we become Christians we are like newborn babies. All the latent character of Christ is in us. That is what is supposed to grow, not the ambitions, habits, and lusts of the old life.

Not only does Jesus share the attributes of divinity; He shares the divine work. He created the universe. "For by Him all things were created, both in the heavens and on earth, visible and invisible, whether thrones or dominions or rulers or authorities—all things have been created by Him and for Him. And He is before all things, and in Him all things hold together" (Col. 1:16–17).

John adds his testimony to that of Paul: "All things came into being by Him, and apart from Him nothing came into being that has come into being" (John 1:13). God the Father was the executive, but Jesus was the agent of creation. "Through [the Son] also He made the world" (Heb. 1:2).

The universal witness of the Bible is that Jesus is God. The Gospels saw Him as God. The prophecy of His birth announced, "'Behold, the virgin shall be with child, and shall bear a Son, and they shall call His name Immanuel,' which translated means, 'God with us'" (Matt. 1:23, quoting Isa. 7:14). His nearness is propitious to us.

The Jews understood His claim: "For this cause therefore the Jews were seeking all the more to kill Him, because He . . . was calling God His own Father, making Himself equal with God" (John 5:18). He claimed for Himself the title of God that had been revealed to Moses in Exodus 3:14: "Truly, truly, I say to you, before Abraham was born, I am" (John 8:58). When Thomas recognized the risen Christ, he exclaimed, "My Lord and my God!" (John 20:28).

The epistles, or New Testament letters, understood Jesus' deity. The hymn that is the subject of this book said, "although He existed in the form of God, [He] did not regard equality with God a thing to be grasped" (Phil. 2:6). Paul declared, "For in Him all the fulness of Deity dwells in bodily form" (Col. 2:9). He told Titus that we are "looking for the blessed hope and the appearing of the glory of our great God and Savior, Christ Jesus" (Titus 2:13). The writer of Hebrews said, "And He is the radiance of [God's] glory and the exact representation of His nature" (Heb. 1:3).

He is the Son of God (Matt. 16:16–17). He has the same nature as the Father. He is the second person in that divine unity that inspired Moses to proclaim God as one (Deut. 6:4). Each member of the Trinity expresses deity in its fullness.

He qualifies for the work of salvation because He is both God and man. Salvation is a mightier work than creation. In creation, Christ did not need to defeat enemies. In accomplishing our salvation, He defeated sin, death, and Satan. John testified, "And we have beheld and bear witness that the Father has sent the Son to be the Savior of the world" (1 John 4:14). He is the creator, but He is also the savior of the world.

Jesus shares in the glory of God: "For God, who said, 'Light shall shine out of darkness,' is the One who has shone in our hearts to give the light of the knowledge of the glory of God in the face of Christ" (2 Cor. 4:6). He is, in short, "Jesus Christ, the Lord of glory" (James 2:1 KJV).

The Assurance That Christ's Deity Gives Us

Jesus is God, and therefore He can do anything God can do. He has all the power of God to do for us what we need. He has all the intentions that God has for us.

Because He is God, Christ can and will protect us. At the time of His arrest, Jesus protected the disciples (John 18:7–9). Protecting us is His nature as our shepherd. Christians have the assurance that He is always with us.

One of Christ's divine functions is to sustain us. In His intercessory prayer, Jesus said of His disciples, "While I was with them, I was keeping them in Thy name which Thou hast given Me; and I guarded them" (John 17:12). Paul too was assured that Christ would guard him (2 Tim. 1:12). Since He is immutable, He does the same work in us that He has done in others.

The Bible assures us that Christ will also complete the process of making us like Himself. John wrote, "Beloved, now we are children of God, and it has not appeared as yet what we shall be. We know that, when He appears, we shall be like Him, because we shall see Him just as He is" (1 John 3:2). Paul wrote the Philippians, "For I am confident of this very thing, that He who began a good work in you will perfect it until the day of Christ Jesus" (Phil. 1:6).

God's right hand is "majestic in power" (Exod. 15:6), and that power is favorable to us. Jesus' intention toward us is that of love, for God is love (1 John 4:8). Paul assures us that both the power of Christ and the love of Christ is the birthright of every believer: "For I am convinced that neither death, nor life, nor angels, nor principalities, nor things present, nor things to come, nor powers, nor height, nor depth, nor any other created thing, shall be able to separate us from the love of God, which is in Christ Jesus our Lord" (Rom. 8:38–39).

Puzzling Paradoxes

A man in Ohio asked me a difficult question. He said, "I do not understand the difference in the two testaments. In the Old Testament, God is so terrifyingly holy that He is constantly telling us to keep our distance. In the New Testament, however, He is warm and loving. There He comes close to us. They are opposite pictures to me. Can those two opposites of holiness and love be reconciled?"

I told him, "Calvary reconciles those two opposites. Nothing like the cross of Christ shows us how holy God really is. The appalling and terrible requirements of God's awesome holiness called for nothing less than the cross to make us holy. At the same time, nothing like the sacrifice of Christ shows us how vast God's love is and how far He is willing to go to reach us in His infinite love."

For two thousand years theologians have struggled with what are apparently two opposite poles (if infinity can have a pole) in God's nature—holiness and love. A closely related polarity consists of the apparent opposites of justice and mercy. Another is that of judgment and grace. On the one side we can group God's holiness, justice, and judgment. On the other side is His love, mercy, and grace.

I checked these words in my thesaurus and found that it listed them indiscriminately under such headings as *divineness* and *God*. To be God is to be holy and just, according to the thesaurus. Yet the same entries said that to be God is to be love—merciful and forgiving. Jesus' example must somehow reconcile these apparently antithetical qualities, since He is God. When we have the mind of Christ, we will have the same qualities on our human level.

In personal encounters with God, people in the Bible saw first His holiness and reacted to it with terror. God told Moses to take off his shoes in the presence of holiness, and Moses hid his face (Exod. 3:5–60). When Isaiah saw God's holiness, he cried, "Woe is me, for I am ruined! Because I am a man of unclean lips, And I live among a people of unclean lips" (Isa. 6:5). God's holiness rouses our fear.

Since Jesus is God, we should expect people to have the same reaction to Him. However, in the incarnation, Jesus' deity was "veiled" in flesh. People rarely recognized His divine character, but sometimes it happened. When Simon Peter realized the terrifying power of Jesus, he pleaded, "Depart from me, for I am a sinful man, O Lord" (Luke 5:8).

Later on Patmos, John saw Him in His divine glory, and "fell at His feet as a dead man" (Rev. 1:17).

We risk irreverence and loss of perspective if we do not begin with the holiness of God. Yet we miss God Himself if we fail to see the immensity of the love revealed through the person of Jesus Christ.

With the paradoxes, the Bible simplifies multidimensional truth so that it becomes comprehensible. With our human limitation we cannot grasp how perfect judgment can show grace. Holiness and love have a relationship, not immediately apparent, that is profound and far-reaching in its implications.

The Bible takes these apparently contradictory qualities for granted. For example, since God is holy, we should expect Him to tell us, "Therefore, come out from their midst and be separate, says the Lord" (2 Cor. 6:17). On the other hand, Jesus made the command that love would make: "Go therefore and make disciples of all the nations" (Matt. 28:19). So holiness commands us to come out of the world, and love commands us to go into the world.

Jesus Himself juxtaposed these contradictions in His intercessory prayer. He said of His disciples, "They are not of the world, even as I am not of the world" (John 17:14). Seconds later He said, "As Thou didst send Me into the world, I have also sent them into the world" (John 17:18). No contradiction existed in the mind of Jesus.

Jesus' own example reconciles the differences. When He said, "I am not of this world" (John 8:23), He was describing the difference in His way of thinking and that of the world. His inner life was separated. He sharply distinguished His thought from that of the prevailing Jewish world, the militaristic Roman world, and the fashionable Greek world.

Yet love is not isolationist. His outer life did indeed go into Galilee, Perea, and Judea; "I must preach the kingdom of God to the other cities also" (Luke 4:43). The outer members of His body served an inner purpose: His feet went, His tongue told, His hands healed. We must separate our inner life from worldly patterns of thought for our outer life to accomplish God's aims. The two poles, instead of being mutually contradictory, are necessary to reveal the complete nature of God.

Jesus told the twelve as they went through Galilee to be "wise as serpents, and harmless as doves" (Matt. 10:16 KJV). Again in Christ we see the resolution of an apparent paradox. Justice requires wisdom; love does no harm. Holiness requires justice. Thus justice denounced the Pharisees (Matt. 23:13–36). Christ's love, on the other hand, showed mercy to the woman who washed His feet (Luke 7:36–50). Justice without mercy or mercy without justice becomes perverted. But the perfect blending of justice and mercy meet in the mind of Christ.

One of the strangest expressions of these opposite poles is seen in two New Testament statements about the will of God and the will of man. If we are to meet the exacting demands of holiness, we should hope that it is Christ in us who meets the standards He requires. Jesus said, "You did not choose Me, but I chose you" (John 15:16). We, the redeemed, are a product of His will. The initiative is His, and therefore the primary responsibility for our personal holiness is His.

On the other hand, if God is also love, He would want our will to cooperate. He wants us to choose Him. We are also told, "Let the one who wishes take the water of life without cost" (Rev. 22:17). Jesus' choice of us reflects the will of God; our choice of Him is the will of man.

Again in Christ we see a compounding of these apparently disparate elements. The will of man—that of Jesus—was identical to the will of God. In the extreme trial of His humanity, He prayed, "My Father, if it is possible, let this cup pass from Me; yet not as I will, but as Thou wilt. . . . My Father, if this cannot pass away unless I drink it, Thy will be done" (Matt. 26:39, 42). The divine interchange shows the divine unity—the Father leading, and Jesus in perfect step with that leading. Jesus' life exhibits holiness and love blended into a perfect unity.

Can We Be Holy and Loving Like Jesus?

We cannot imitate deity. Believers increasingly have the mind of Christ, but they will never become divine. None of us will ever be all-knowing or all-wise. Yet Christ's life illustrates these characteristic poles in a human way for our example. The *human* manifestations are for our imitation.

The mind of Christ is holy. Hebrews tells us that "it was fitting that we should have such a high priest, holy, innocent, undefiled, separated from sinners and exalted above the heavens" (Heb. 7:26). The universal testimony of the Bible is that Christ is holy. We are to have His mind, and that mind is holy.

Jesus expressed His desire that we be holy. He prayed, "And for their sakes I sanctify Myself, that they themselves also may be sanctified in truth" (John 17:19). He was praying for His disciples, but in the next verse He indicated that He included all who would follow afterward in His prayer.

The Bible uses the word *sanctify* to mean that people set something apart. They regard the object as holy, or they treat it as holy. For example, the Jews were commanded, "Remember the sabbath day, to keep it holy" (Exod. 20:8).

All believers are holy. We are sanctified by faith in Christ (Acts 26:18). Paul wrote of Christians, "But you were washed, but you were sanctified, but you were justified in the name of the Lord Jesus Christ, and in the power of our God" (1 Cor. 6:11). Holiness is the natural state of the Christian.

Yet we have a responsibility—we are also to perfect this holiness (2 Cor. 7:1). We are to grow in it. "This is the will of God, your sanctification; that is, that you abstain from sexual immorality, that each of you know how to possess his own vessel in sanctification and honor" (1 Thess. 4:3). We are to participate in the process.

An immediate project, one that you could do today, is to dedicate your body to the Lord. As used in the Bible, the word *dedicate* means that something has been set aside for God. Sanctification is God's responsibility, but dedication is our work.

Paul wrote the Roman Christians, "I urge you therefore, brethren, by the mercies of God, to present your bodies a living and holy sacrifice, acceptable to God, which is your spiritual service of worship" (Rom. 12:1). If my body belongs to God, it will be holy, for that is what the word *holy* means—set apart for God.

So that I would never mistake "presenting my body to God" and so that I would never forget what I had done, I went to my prayer closet and dedicated my body to the Lord, part by part. I started with my feet and told the Lord, "They will never go anywhere You would not want them to go. They will be Your servants to take me where You direct." I dedicated my stomach, my lungs, my hands, my mouth—every part of my body.

I urge you to do the same. Dedicating the parts of your body becomes a memorable experience. It is a major step in having the mind of Christ. I felt it a relief to know that I no longer belonged to myself, but to God. My body—my seeing, my hearing, my digestion—is now God's responsibility. However, I do not blame God for the accidents that happen in the environment of a fallen humanity—food poisoning, viruses, declining faculties, or a stubbed toe. If you will take this step, God will have moved you a long way toward perfecting holiness.

If our lives are to demonstrate holiness and justice, they also are to show love, mercy, and grace. Our guide to the biblical expression of love is in 1 Corinthians 13:4–7. Carrying out the expression of love in those four verses requires thoughtful and prayerful diligence. The person who wants the mind of Christ will meditate on these fifteen actions.

Yet the highest expression of love is in the sacrificial giving of ourselves. Jesus' life was a life of sacrifice, of self-giving. He "made himself of no reputation" (Phil. 2:7 KJV). The Master who created the universe "continued in subjection to [His earthly parents]" (Luke 2:51). He temporarily sacrificed authority. He who was king above all kings became an itinerant preacher. He sacrificed nobility. The wonder-worker who fed thousands gave up food to concentrate on His Father's will. He sacrificed bodily satisfaction. He sacrificed heaven to come to us. If love is self-giving, Jesus is love.

Jesus' entire life was a pattern of continuing self-sacrifice. With that pattern established, a time came when He could offer His life as a sacrifice for our sins. "Greater love has no one than this, that one lay down his life for his friends" (John 15:13). His lifelong practice culminated in the noblest of all sacrifices.

Jesus' life is our pattern, but we should not start with the big sacrifices. We cannot make the grand sacrifices with the nobility of spirit that Christ had. So we do better to start with small sacrifices.

Most of us are not accustomed to sacrifices, however small. We expect a return for our effort, for our payments. We know little of giving without receiving.

Jesus said that blessing lay in unexpectant giving (Acts 20:35). Paul agrees. His sacrifices were not a loss: "But whatever things were gain to me, those things I have counted as loss for the sake of Christ. More than that, I count all things to be loss in view of the surpassing value of knowing Christ Jesus my Lord, for whom I have suffered the loss of all things, and count them but rubbish in order that I may gain Christ" (Phil. 3:7–8). Paul had the mind of Christ.

Love will make the sacrifices. In doing so, it will discover the happiness of giving. You can make that same discovery. I urge you to begin small. Sacrificial giving is a grace we can grow in.

Start by giving to the Lord. Give Him something that costs you effort, time, or money. Find one of His causes that interests you, or a church, or a mission effort. You may give in small increments at first (only an hour or a little money). God will bless that. Continue your giving, and you will discover a desire to broaden it. Give out of love for the Lord.

As the Lord broadens your joy in giving, give to people. Try doing small favors. In my experience, when we do a favor or give a gift secretly, we amplify the joy. Love is generous and needs no credit. This, however, may take a period of growth. In time, sacrificial giving becomes such a joy that it becomes a way of life.

It was a way of life with Christ. He is God, and God is love. The Gospels mention various emotions in the accounts of Jesus' life, but the most frequently mentioned emotion is love (for example, Mark 10:21; John 11:5; 13:1, 34). If we are to have the mind of Christ, we must live holy lives and love as Jesus loved. By slowly making small sacrifices, we may grow to the point where we can make the grand ones.

Conclusion

The image I am conforming to is that of God in flesh. His deity assures me that Christ will take care of me and will finish the process of conforming me to His image. As God, He carries the apparent polarities of holiness and love. As human and with His help, I also will be holy and loving. He will help me in His position as God.

chapter six

A Servant

But made himself of no reputation,
and took upon him the form of a servant.

At first, I thought he was showing special deference just to me. He worked hard to help me find a retirement house. He watched our house and cared for it in the year of our absence before we moved into it. He saw that the lawn was mowed. When I mentioned painting the closets, he recruited church members to do it, and then worked with them. It seemed that I could not mention a need without him hurrying to fulfill that need.

Then I moved to his town and joined his church. His name was Lucian Stohler, and soon I discovered that his name was synonymous with service. He continued to attend to me and my family, but now I became aware that he attended to everybody. He met needs quietly and without officiousness. He was constantly available and working on behalf of others. People in the church had the attitude, "If you really want to get something done, call on Lucian."

I asked Lucian to tell me what brought this attitude into his life. He said that a crisis led him to dedicate his life and his whole personality to servanthood. He led a "normal" Christian life until a pastor's retreat in Michigan brought a confrontation with his life purposes. The preacher, Tommy Jones, spoke on the deeper life in such a way that Lucian realized the importance of the lordship of Christ. He struggled with that concept. He mentioned this to Tommy, who said, "You know what to do." Lucian went to the back bedroom of his cabin and poured out his heart to the Lord.

He realized that he had been angry with the Lord because God had not given him a wife. He said he "regurgitated" all the bitterness he had at God. He told me that the hardest words he ever said were the words he said that day: "Lord, if your lordship means I'll never be married, I accept your lordship."

In the three years before he met his wife, the Lord taught him the meaning of servanthood. He learned the walk of ministry, which is to say, the walk of a life given to the service of others. He learned that ministry and servanthood were synonymous. His own words were, "My drive to serve has given me a love for people that makes me want to help them, to serve them, and to witness the love of Christ to them." For Lucian Stohler, lordship meant servanthood. He also helped me understand that concept.

To have the mind of Christ is to be a servant. The entire Christ story is the story of a servant. The great Messianic passages predicted Him as a servant: "Behold, My Servant, whom I uphold; My chosen one in whom My soul delights" (Isa. 42:1). The suffering servant of Isaiah 53 was a "righteous servant": "As a result of the anguish of His soul, He will see it and be satisfied; By His knowledge the Righteous One, My Servant, will justify the many, As He will bear their iniquities" (Isa. 53:11).

Unlike the world system, in Christ's kingdom, servanthood, not position, is the key to greatness. Here spiritual stature is implicit in servanthood. After Salome requested that James and John sit at Jesus' right and left hand in His kingdom, He told the indignant disciples: "You know that the rulers of the Gentiles lord it over them, and their great men exercise authority over them. It is not so among you, but whoever wishes to become great among you shall be your servant, and whoever wishes to be first among you shall be your slave; just as the Son of Man did not come to be served, but to serve, and to give His life a ransom for many" (Matt. 20:25–28).

We've Never Done It That Way Before

This surprisingly reverses all the values we have learned on earth. Yet it could not be any other way if heaven is to be heaven. The unity of spirit Jesus expects in His body is impossible in a stratified society of important and unimportant persons, such as the earthly society we live in.

Genuine oneness of spirit is feasible only if every member in society is submissive to all the others. Only in a universally submissive society would rivalry be impossible. But we cannot imagine a world with no rivalry. In such a world, joy would come from the privilege of service, and that is available only to the lowly. The last, astonishingly, are first, and the least really are the greatest.

Such a society would have only one supreme authority, and Jesus tells us, "No servant can serve two masters; for either he will hate the one, and love the other, or else he will hold to one, and despise the other" (Luke 16:13). God is supreme. We can please only one Master—Jesus. The servant Paul knew this lesson. He wrote, "Am I now seeking the favor of men, or of God? Or am I striving to please men? If I were still trying to please men, I would not be a bond-servant of Christ" (Gal. 1:10).

We do serve Christ supremely, but we are also to serve one another. "You were called to freedom, brethren; only do not turn your freedom into an opportunity for the flesh, but through love serve one another" (Gal. 5:13). If this appears contradictory—we are to serve only Christ and yet we also are to serve one another—the solution is that we are not to serve each other as master.

Our mutual service is an act of love and mutual submission, not of mutual obedience (although we obey constituted authority). Our obedience is to Christ while we serve one another. These two commands—serve Christ as master and serve one another in love—follow the order in the command to love God above all else and to love our neighbor as ourself.

The biblical relationship of servant to master was often intimate. The Lord compares it to that of a father and son in Malachi 1:6: "A son honors his father, and a servant his master." Jesus compares it to that of a student and his teacher in Matthew 10:25: "It is enough for the disciple that he become as his teacher, and the slave as his master."

The centurion in Matthew 8:5–13 loved his servant; without that love he would not have contacted Jesus. In the Old Testament, the servant Eliezer's careful obedience to Abraham (Gen. 24:1–61) shows an uncommon depth of relationship. Intimacy is necessary if master and servant are to realize their common goal. The whole tenor of the New Testament indicates that Jesus expects an intimate relationship between Himself and His servants.

God gives special protection for His servants. "'No weapon that is formed against you shall prosper; And every tongue that accuses you in judgment you will condemn. This is the heritage of the servants of the LORD, And their vindication is from Me,' declares the LORD" (Isa. 54:17). God assures us, "The hand of the LORD shall be made known to His servants" (Isa. 66:14). Being a servant enlists His protection and His provision.

How Does Jesus Define Servanthood?

Thirteen of Jesus' parables mention servants. In six of these, the principal thrust is servanthood. The first of these to consider is Matthew 25:14–30, the parable of the talents. Two men invested their master's money well and doubled his return. One man buried his talent. The master commended the industrious servants, but called the one who buried his talent "wicked" and "lazy."

The master incidentally showed wisdom in the number of talents he gave each man. The two men entrusted with the greater quantity of money worked harder, and the untrustworthy servant lived up to the small estimate of the master. Jesus was saying that He expects initiative and hard work from His servants.

In this parable, Jesus said, "For to everyone who has shall more be given, and he shall have an abundance; but from the one who does not have, even what he does have shall be taken away" (Matt. 25:29; see also Luke 19:26). If greatness lies in service, we need to remember that the more service we undertake, the more God will give us. If God gives us much to do, He will expect more from us, but in that process we can increase our own treasure in heaven. Both advantage and risk are found in larger opportunity. The more we serve, the more we increase our opportunities—but we dare not waste them.

The second parable on servanthood is Mark 13:34–37. A master left his servants in charge of his house with assigned tasks and told them to be watchful for his return. The master expected to find the servants working and watching when he returned.

In the third parable, Luke 12:35–40, Jesus describes the servants ready and watching for the return of the master. The emphasis of this parable is not on work as such, but rather on the expectation in the mind of the servants waiting for the return of the master. One part of our work is simply to watch.

The fourth parable, Luke 12:42–48, treats readiness for service. Again the master leaves the servants in charge of his house. Jesus contrasts the watchfulness of the good servants with the negligence of the servants who beat the others and became drunk. The expectation of the servant is his continuing alertness in carrying out his instructions.

In this parable, Jesus said, "From everyone who has been given much shall much be required; and to whom they entrusted much, of him they will ask all the more" (Luke 12:48). In the parable of the talents, the five-talent man had more demanded of him. What if he had buried the five talents? The waste would have been much more serious than that in the burying of the one talent.

In the fifth parable, Luke 17:7–10, Jesus asks a rhetorical question: Will the master thank a servant for carrying out his orders? In verse 10, He tells us that mere obedience is not worthy of the name *servant*. He is saying that a worthy servant will go beyond duty.

The sixth parable is the parable of the minas (Luke 19:12–27). Similar to the parable of the talents, in this one the master gives the various servants an equal amount, but their performance differs radically. The master shows his wisdom, not by entrusting appropriate amounts to the servants, but rather by the justness of the rewards he gives to them. Again Jesus is indicating that He will reward hard work and initiative.

In five of these servanthood parables, the master is absent. The time of the master's return is unknown, and in every case he comes at an unexpected moment. The emphasis is on the servant's performance while the master is absent. Three qualities are emphasized: initiative, readiness to obey, and watchfulness.

Seven other parables mention servants and shed incidental light on the first-century role of servants. They are: Matthew 13:24–30 (the parable of the tares or weeds), Matthew 18:23–35 (the parable of the unforgiving servant), Matthew 20:1–15 (a landowner hired men to work in his vineyard all day), Matthew 21:33–40 (an absent master sent slaves to collect the rent), Matthew 22:2–13 (a king sent slaves to call invited guests to a wedding feast), Luke 15:22 (part of the parable of the prodigal son in which the servants were bidden to bring clothing), and Luke 16:1–8 (the parable of the unjust steward or manager).

From these we see that first-century masters expected their servants to do many menial tasks: gather and burn useless weeds and collect wheat into a barn (Matt. 13:30), call invited guests to a wedding feast (Matt. 22:3), bind an improperly dressed wedding guest and throw him out (Matt. 22:13), bring clothing and kill a fatted calf (Luke 15:22–23), plow and tend sheep (Luke 17:7), and serve food (Luke 17:8). God may expect us to do lowly, ignoble tasks. The servant does not choose his work, the master does.

On the other hand, the master could assign highly responsible jobs. Four times the parables mention tasks that involve authority: collect rent (Matt. 21:34), be in charge of a household (Matt. 24:45), and invest money (Matt. 25:14–30; Luke 19:12–27). Abraham sent Eliezer to get a bride for Isaac (Gen. 24:2–4). God may call upon His servants to do the lowest or the highest tasks.

In four of the parables, the servants are pictured as taking initiative and even volunteering service. In Matthew 13:27–28, the servants reported to the master after an enemy sowed weeds in his crop. The servants volunteered to pull them up. In another parable, a rich man demanded an accounting of an unjust manager. The manager excused large portions of the debts of his master's debtors (Luke 16:5–7), and so ingratiated himself with the debtors. The master commended his shrewdness. In the parables of the talents and the minas, the servants invested money.

Initiative and shrewdness are commendable within the confines of obedience, both in the menial tasks of the parable of the weeds and in the responsible tasks of the parables of the talents and minas. Also implicit in these is that the good servants worked diligently.

Imitating Jesus, The Righteous Servant

From Jesus' parables, we understand the qualities that He emphasized as essential to servanthood. Those qualities are watchfulness, obedience, initiative, hard work, shrewdness, and going beyond duty.

Watchfulness

Watchfulness was the one quality most emphasized in Jesus' teaching on servanthood. Biblical servants were watchful. The psalmist said, "Behold, as the eyes of servants look to the hand of their master, As the eyes of a maid to the hand of her mistress; So our eyes look to the LORD our God, Until He shall be gracious to us" (Ps. 123:2).

We cannot be obedient until we are watchful. We are to be watchful for Christ's return (as He said), but we also should be alert to the leading of the Lord in our daily lives.

That degree of watchfulness is difficult to maintain, but Jesus did. His eyes were continually on His Father. After His initiative at the healing of Bethesda, He told the Jews, "My Father is working until now, and I Myself am working" (John 5:17). When they objected to this claim to equality with the Father, He emphasized where His attention lay: "Truly, truly, I say to you, the Son can do nothing of Himself, unless it is something He sees the Father doing; for whatever the Father does, these things the Son also does in like manner" (John 5:19). He was watchful, or attentive, vertically to the Father.

Jesus' watchfulness was deliberate. Here we see the Will Principle of chapter 1 demonstrated in Jesus' life. He spent the night before He chose His disciples in prayer (John 6:12). By communing with His Father, He determined which of His followers would recognize and obey His authority. The most important ingredient in watchfulness is prayer.

Another ingredient is alertness. Christ was alert vertically, and He was also alert horizontally to His fellow man. He was sensitive to a woman who touched His garments (Mark 5:25–34). Although she tried to escape attention, He singled her out and commended her faith. His sensitivity to the paralytic lowered through the roof caused Him to deal with the man's sinful condition before He healed him (Mark 2:5).

To develop the quality of watchfulness in your life, it is urgent that your prayer life grow. This means that as you progress through each day, you will be constantly turning to God to know His direction. Learn to shoot "arrow" prayers to God constantly. While I am in conversation, I ask for help in discerning what kind of opportunity the conversation affords to glorify God or to minister to my fellows. At work, remain in contact with God. Throughout your day God is your constant reference point.

To be watchful is simply to be available. An employer has the right to expect his employees to be available. The employee (or the servant) is at the disposition of the employer (or the master). The superior should be able to call on the servant at any moment (as people called on Lucian Stohler).

We must be available, first to God and then to others. Some distractions that come our way may really be an opportunity for service. My telephone rings incessantly. When this began to happen, it annoyed me. I thought it was a distraction from "more important" duties. As I studied the example of Christ, I found countless distractions in His life. Yet He was available to the needy. They could always count on His attention. I had to learn, somewhat painfully, that servants always remain available.

We can facilitate this kind of watchfulness by having a daily time of prayer alone with the Lord. Jesus prayed in the early morning (Mark 1:35), but you may need to do yours at some other time of the day if your body clock so dictates.

Obedience

Jesus was obedient. He claimed, "For I have come down from heaven, not to do My own will, but the will of Him who sent Me" (John 6:38). His incarnation is itself an act of obedience. Because He was watchful, He knew the commands of His Father. His entire life is a record of total obedience. At the end of His life, He could confidently assert, "As the Father gave Me commandment, even so I do" (John 14:31). That allegiance led to Gethsemane, with its struggle, and to the cross.

Obedience is one part of the mind of Christ that is solely your responsibility. No one can obey for you. Try keeping a record of the times when you know you were obedient. Obedience is total, or it is not genuine obedience. We cannot choose when we will obey if we have the biblical quality of obedience as Christ had it.

Initiative

Jesus often took initiative. Although the majority of His healings were in response to requests, He often initiated a healing. In Peter's home, He chose to heal Peter's mother-in-law (Matt. 8:14–17). His healing on the Sabbath of a man with a withered hand occasioned the Pharisees' plot to put Him to death (Mark 3:1–6).

We would not have the mind of Christ if we were not aware that all His initiatives were at the disposition of His Father. Although He often initiated an action, He claimed, "I can do nothing on My own initiative. As I hear, I judge; and My judgment is just, because I do not seek My own will, but the will of Him who sent Me" (John 5:30). In His sensitivity to His Father, He started projects, miracles, and events as His Father led Him. His initiatives were with those subordinate to Him or with the needy and at the direction of His Father.

Some of these initiatives led to confrontations with His enemies. When He healed the woman bent double for eighteen years, the synagogue ruler objected to a Sabbath healing (Luke 13:10–17). Jesus began another Sabbath healing while a confrontation was already in progress (Luke 14:1–6).

He approached the sick man at the pool of Bethesda and asked if he wanted to be healed. This too led to a confrontation over the Sabbath (John 5:1–17). Still another Sabbath conflict arose when He healed the man born blind (John 9:1–41). The evidence indicates that He intended to provoke the confrontations. In these initiatives, He was using the Sabbath for the good of man.

In some of His nonhealing miracles, Jesus took the initiative. He instigated the miraculous catch of fish that induced Peter, James, and John (and probably Andrew) to leave everything and follow Him (Luke 5:4–11). His feeding of the five thousand was not prompted by any visible factor (Mark 6:35–44). It was out of the initiative of compassion.

Time and again Jesus assumed the initiative in His life and ministry. He had to convince John the Baptist to baptize Him (Matt. 3:13–17). In Matthew 16:13–20, He elicited from Peter the famous confession of faith.

Our initiative must be of the same kind if we are to have the mind of Christ. Several years ago I became aware that a strong potential source for evangelism was available to missionaries through the medium of music. I prayed much, and through the leadership of the Lord, I pioneered a course at a seminary called "Music in Missions." Nothing like this had ever existed before. Hundreds of missionaries have now been through the course and are using the techniques to attract otherwise hostile persons to the gospel through music.

Start seeking opportunities to start projects for God. If you are alert, these may involve ministry to the sick or the troubled—like Jesus' initiatives. You may see an opportunity to teach or to share; He did. We always bend our initiatives to the direction of God's will. Jesus' initiatives were at the direction of His Father. Again, no one ever had the mind of Christ without much prayer.

Hard Work

Jesus worked hard. Early in His ministry, the famous "busy day" saw Him starting the day by calling four disciples (Mark 1:16–20), instigating a miraculous catch of fish (Luke 5:1–7), teaching in the synagogue of Capernaum (Mark 1:21–22), casting out a demon (vv. 23–27), healing Simon's mother-in-law (vv. 29–31), and then healing multitudes during the evening hours (vv. 32–34). He must have been exhausted after such a grueling day, and yet "in the early morning, while it was still dark, He arose and went out and departed to a lonely place, and was praying there" (Mark 1:35).

His life was full. The constant circuits across and around Galilee, His availability to the maimed and impaired, and His perpetual teaching all mark a life of hard work. He never wasted time, dawdled, or procrastinated.

Nor can we if we are to have His mind. This does not mean that we cannot have occasional leisure times. Jesus attempted occasional withdrawals (Matt. 15:21; Mark 3:7), although persons usually interrupted Him (Matt. 15:22–28; Mark 3:8–9). When He withdrew, He remained available to the needy. Even in His withdrawals, we find Him working. If we are watchful and obedient, we will work hard, but we may occasionally withdraw.

Shrewdness

Shrewdness characterized Jesus' dealings with His enemies. Normally Jesus did His miracles in Galilee and had His following there. However, He raised Lazarus from the dead in Judea, where His enemies headquartered. This miracle caused their decision to put Him to death. Jesus did not fear death, but He knew that His death must occur at Passover. He was the Passover lamb (John 1:29). To avoid a premature death, He slipped back up into Ephraim, to await Passover week (John 11:53). When the time came to die, He marched boldly into Jerusalem (probably about three weeks later; John 12:12–18). He did not fear death, but He wisely determined its timing.

Most of us will have difficulty determining to be shrewd, but we can use the wits that we have. This depends partly on our alertness. We can pray for God to give us a godly wisdom.

Going Beyond Duty

In the parable of the servant attending to the master before attending to his personal needs, Jesus emphasized that servants must go beyond duty (Luke 17:7–10). Obedience is not enough if we are to qualify for the mind of Christ. He ended the parable by saying, "So you too, when you do all the things which are commanded you, say, 'We are unworthy slaves; we have done only that which we ought to have done'" (Luke 17:10).

That He was always available shows His willingness to go beyond duty. That He cared for the needs of Judas shows that He would go beyond duty. He knew from the beginning that Judas was a traitor (John 6:64). Significantly, His warning to Judas came a full year before Judas's betrayal (John 6:70). He did more than He needed to do to be obedient.

The consummate example of going beyond duty is the cross. Death is the highest penalty anyone can pay. "He laid down His life for us" (1 John 3:16). His life is our measure.

A Servant

This attitude—going beyond duty—is the highest challenge we have yet met in our attempt to have the mind of Christ. Peter issues the challenge: "Therefore, since Christ has suffered in the flesh, arm yourselves also with the same purpose" (1 Pet. 4:1, the Greek here is perhaps better translated as "mind").

We have the word of Scripture that beyond the suffering is joy. "For the joy set before Him [He] endured the cross" (Heb. 12:2). Service leads to joy. We saw above that the reward for service is greater opportunity for service (Matt. 25:29). Being a servant is one of the loftiest privileges of the Christian life. Serving God and others is the mind of Christ.

Note how indispensable each quality of servanthood is to the other. We cannot obey without being watchful. We cannot take the proper initiative if we are not obedient. Our hard work grows out of watchfulness and obedience. Shrewdness or godly wisdom should characterize all our work. We must be industrious if we are to go beyond duty. The qualities, again, are integrated.

Below is a list of actions and attitudes we will cultivate to have the servant mind. These attitudes will only develop if we remain in prayer about them. Ask the Lord to cultivate within you these actions and attitudes.

Actions	Attitudes
Watchfulness	1. I pray daily about my service.
	2. I pray often throughout the day to seek direction from the Lord.
	3. I am attentive to needs as they arise around me.
	4. I am available to people when they express a need to me.
Obedience	5. I am obeying all known commands of Scripture.
	6. I will be glad to do menial tasks or highly responsible tasks.
	7. Right now I am in the center of God's will for me.
	8. I commit myself totally to the will of God. This means that I know that tomorrow I will do God's will, whatever it is.
Initiative	9. I will promptly move into any new area of service the Lord directs me.
	10. I will be courageous about investing talent, work, or money, as the Lord leads me.

Hard work	11. I determine not to dawdle or to procrastinate as the Lord guides me.
	12. I do all my presently assigned work "heartily, as for the Lord rather than for men" (Col. 3:23).
Shrewdness	13. I will constantly pray that God will help me keep my wits about me.
	14. I will try to use God's method about my work rather than my own method.
Going beyond duty	15. My primary incentive is the glory of Christ.
	16. I do not set limits on the privilege of service.

Conclusion

Christ's servant mind in me facilitates the mental quality of alertness. God's goal is the kingdom business. For that business, I will be watchful, obedient, creative, and industrious. I will use God's method and will draw no limits on God's expectation of me. I can measure my growth in servanthood only by Christ's obedience. He enables my servanthood in His office as Master. He leads me.

chapter seven

A Man

and was made in the likeness of men:
And being found in fashion as a man

*I*n chapter 1, we saw that humans are made in God's image. The New Testament picks up this emphasis and requires that we become like Christ. Not even the angels are made in God's image. God made man in His image so that He could become human. He did not become an angel.

In the future life, redeemed humans will judge the angels (1 Cor. 6:3). They will reign with Christ (Rev. 5:10). These two facts tell us that regenerate humanity is the nobility of the universe. Redeemed humanity will someday be the highest ranking of all creatures, even above the angels. From the beginning, God intended our Christlikeness. Redeemed and perfected humanity is God's highest creation.

Whatever glory we finally attain, God will use our time on earth to prepare us for that unimaginable reign. His training program to prepare us is found in the Sermon on the Mount. The basic principles of living to please God are spelled out in that sermon. In these three chapters, Jesus tells us what redeemed humans are to be and what kind of behavior pleases God.

The old covenant was based on law. The new covenant is based on the redemptive work of Christ for us. The Old Testament law dealt with physical matters. It was to be obeyed strictly. The Sermon on the Mount deals with the spirit and with attitudes. It is concerned with principles, rather than restrictions. We obey its principles by conforming to its spirit.

Jesus introduces His sermon with eight blessings, or beatitudes (Matt. 5:3–12). These beatitudes set the framework for the attitudes and actions in the teaching that follows. They are symmetrical. Between the first four and the last four, they establish a balance in the way God will work in our lives and the way we will work in God's kingdom. Each beatitude contains a principle about the way God works in us.

The First Four Beatitudes: Our Need of God

The first four beatitudes are closely related. In them we experience an atmosphere of neediness and dependence. They progress sequentially in this atmosphere to a climax of need in the fourth blessing. Jesus' purpose in blessing us in these ways is to show us our need of God and our dependence on Him. If we apply the principles in each of the attitudes, we end with a profound dependence on God.

The Poor in Spirit

Jesus began these blessings by saying, "Blessed are the poor in spirit, for theirs is the kingdom of heaven." The principle He is introducing is our need of God. Our poverty is spiritual, and our most important need is God. Without God, we are totally insufficient. This need is the appropriate starting place for everything else Jesus is going to say.

We begin the Christian life by being poor in spirit. Only the poor in spirit are willing to repent of their sins. To be repentant is to be poor in spirit. The poor in spirit know that redemption from their sins depends on God alone.

Even after salvation, we continue to be poor, whether we know it or not. One indication of our poverty is that we retain our tendency to sin. We are poor also because we keep our tendency to make mistakes. We are not yet perfect. Other indications of our poverty are our limitations—physical, mental, and spiritual. These indications of poverty are mainly spiritual, for we are all poor in spirit.

Many of us do not recognize our poverty. Jesus wrote the church at Laodicea, "You say, 'I am rich, and have become wealthy, and have need of nothing, and you do not know that you are wretched and miserable and poor and blind and naked" (Rev. 3:17). We can be rich in material wealth without realizing our poverty in spirit.

God may use a painful circumstance to make us acknowledge our insufficiency. He did with me. After the renewal experience described in chapter 5, my relations to a group of people were profoundly affected. I began to experience a number of rejections by persons who were repelled by the change in me. At times I was disheartened. Dejection may become a part of being poor in spirit. I realized that I needed to depend on God more than before. God may allow circumstances to show us our poverty.

The opposite of being poor in spirit is to be proud in spirit. The Lord described a Pharisee proud in spirit. He prayed, "God, I thank Thee that I am not like other people: swindlers, unjust, adulterers, or even like this tax-gatherer. I fast twice a week; I pay tithes of all that I get" (Luke 18:11–12). He relied on his performance. Proud people are self-reliant; they are satisfied and think they lack nothing.

The Lord then described a man who was poor in spirit. "The tax-gatherer, standing some distance away, was even unwilling to lift up his eyes to heaven, but was beating his breast, saying, 'God, be merciful to me, the sinner!'" (Luke 18:13). This tax gatherer was probably not poor in money; he was rich. Yet he was poor in spirit.

The poor in spirit know that they are helpless and incomplete. They know that all their righteousness is borrowed. Whatever work they do, they always start from ground zero. They depend completely on the Lord. The poor in spirit know their profound need.

Being poor in spirit is the first step in turning us into spiritual beings. God is the most important factor in the lives of the poor in spirit. Recognizing our poverty helps us get rid of our ego problem. An inflated ego is a serious obstacle to spiritual progress. When we are truly poor in spirit, the spiritual world becomes more important to us than the material or physical world.

Although Jesus created this universe, in His incarnation He worked from ground zero. He was poor in spirit. He said, "Truly, truly, I say to you, the Son can do nothing of Himself, unless it is something He sees the Father doing" (John 5:19). He did not work independently; He depended on His Father. Later He emphasized, "I can do nothing on My own initiative" (John 5:30). Still later, talking to the Jews, He returned to the same theme: "I do nothing on My own initiative, but I speak these things as the Father taught Me" (John 8:28).

Jesus worked from ground zero because that is what we must do. The poor in spirit need God, and Jesus showed us what it meant to live as though we depended totally on God. That is the mind of Christ for human lives.

Those Who Mourn

Jesus' next beatitude was, "Blessed are those who mourn, for they shall be comforted." The principle of this beatitude is brokenness. Broken people are never flippant or insolent, but they are open to whatever work God wants to do.

Several years ago our daughter, Melana, was ready to enroll for her sophomore year at Texas Christian University. The university allowed us to pay her tuition in three monthly payments. As the first month progressed, we became increasingly anxious when all our fervent praying did not bring the money.

When the bill came, I prayed, "Lord, now I have to pray for two payments. Make something big happen!" Right away our daughter was in an accident, and the insurance did not cover the hospital and the doctor bills.

Now I was discouraged, not because of our bills, but because God was not answering prayer. He did not speak, even when I spent hours searching the Bible. The next month, the second envelope contained a notice that the entire tuition was due. Once again we cried out to the Lord. This time our daughter developed an abscessed tooth. The bill was three hundred dollars, and we had no dental insurance.

Our financial distress was not as painful as the apparent silence of God. In my desperation, I cried to the Lord, "My God, my God, why hast Thou forsaken me?" Even that brought no answer, and so I said to the Lord, "If I cannot hear You speak, I ask you to take me out of the seminary."

Because of the seriousness of this request, I felt I should share with my wife what I had prayed, so that night I told her. Laverne began to weep and confessed, "This is not your fault, it is mine. I'm the one with no faith. I just can't take hold of God as Father."

The pain I felt now was more critical than before. Her home had been split by a divorce while she was young. She had experienced considerable pain from the separation from her father. I cried to the Lord to give me a word for Laverne, and He did. I told her, "Honey, if you can't get hold of God as Father, concentrate on the Lord Jesus and on my love for you. He loves His bride. You are my bride, and I love you."

Laverne brightened at that and said, "Now that is something I can get hold of." I had memorized Ephesians 5, and the Lord used verses 25–33 to introduce a new insight into my home life. I knew that the father in the home gave children their concept of God, but the Lord now made me realize that the husband can help his wife develop a biblical concept of Christ.

The Holy Spirit chose a time of brokenness to illuminate my desperate search. What does a mourner need? He needs comfort, and

Comforter is the name of the third person of the Trinity. Brokenness is the key to the deeper work of the Holy Spirit.

A few days later I remarked casually to Laverne, "As bad as the Lord needs missionaries, I wonder why He won't let us be missionaries?" We had had a continuing desire to go to Spain. When Laverne asked if I was praying about it, I told her that since the Lord had made it plain that I was to teach missions I was not going to talk to the Lord about rebellion. She said, "If you can't talk to the Lord about something so close to your heart, you should stop telling people that He is a friend."

I suddenly realized that I had grossly underestimated the stature of my friend. He invites us to sup with Him (Rev. 3:20). I made two cups of bouillon and spent an hour telling the Lord about my love for missions. In the process, I realized how important the techniques I was teaching were to many missionaries. I felt as though the Lord was speaking directly to me as a friend. As a friend, He assured me of my understanding of His call.

I dreaded the arrival of the last bill from the university. When it came, I could not open it. My wife and daughter did not open it either. We walked around it most of the weekend. When Melana finally read it, she screamed. I came running, and she told me, "Read that letter!" The letter said, "This is to inform you that a friend who wishes to remain anonymous has paid your daughter's tuition for the semester." Soon the Lord enabled us to pay the doctors, the hospital, and the dentist.

Later I prayerfully tried to determine the cause of our financial and spiritual difficulties that fall. In those prayers, I realized that God had used brokenness for our spiritual progress. We learned new insights and new assurance of His care. This was the first time I understood the positive achievements of brokenness.

Later the Lord allowed more difficult breakings to take us deeper into our dependence on the Holy Spirit: an advanced cancer, a death in the family, a separation, and more serious financial reversals. In these later breakings, we learned that brokenness can accomplish much. It purifies, it teaches, and it brings the Comforter into new depths of personal relationship with us.

Jesus knew brokenness in the sense of useful sorrow. He was a "man of sorrows, and acquainted with grief" (Isa. 53:3). He wept over Jerusalem (Luke 19:41; Matt. 23:37–39). His life and mind are proof that brokenness under God's direction leads to wholeness.

The result of breakings in many Christians is bitterness and recrimination. That is not the mind of Christ. God intends to use our misfortune to bring ultimate blessing. Our mishaps may appear to be reversals. God is watching our attitude, and if we look to Him, He will guide us into blessing, even in the hard situations of life.

The Meek

Jesus' third blessing was, "Blessed are the meek, for they shall inherit the earth" (KJV). We saw in chapter 4 that meekness is humility coupled with strength. The principle behind this blessing is submission.

Our primary submission is to God (James 4:7). He has a plan for each life (Eph. 2:10). We submit ourselves to God's direction. The fact that only one person in each Testament is called "meek" (Moses and Jesus; see chapter 4) indicates that God's view of meekness is high indeed. Few people achieve the biblical concept of meekness. We are not fully submitted to God.

My experience in learning God's will is that the better I know Him, the deeper and more far-reaching my submission becomes. He requires more of me today than He did when He first called me to a separated life. I submit to God, and He supplies the strength.

We also submit to others. We submit to human authorities (1 Pet. 2:13–14). Within the body of Christ, we submit to one another (1 Cor. 16:16). In submission, we discover that we need one another. Meekness enables us to admit our need.

Jesus was meek. He submitted to His parents (Luke 2:51), to baptism (Matt. 3:13–15), and to the temple tax (Matt. 17:24–27). It is the basis for His invitation to us to share His burden (Matt. 11:29 KJV). He entered Jerusalem in meekness (Matt. 21:5 KJV). Meekness is the mind of Christ.

Those Who Hunger and Thirst for Righteousness

The fourth of the beatitudes blesses those who are spiritually hungry. The principle is that of yearning. Our greatest single need is for the righteousness of God, and we are blessed when that need so fills our mind that it becomes a yearning.

Most of the New Testament passages on righteousness concern the believer's imputed righteousness in Christ (Rom. 4:6, 11; 1 Cor. 1:30). God credits us with the righteousness of Christ. One of the Old Testament prophecies had declared that Messiah's name would be "The LORD our righteousness" (Jer. 23:6). Since it is Christ's righteousness that we have (not our own), our yearning for righteousness is really our desiring Christ Himself.

Yearning is an intense emotion. Christ's metaphors, *hunger* and *thirst,* indicate an acute consciousness of need. Later in the Sermon on the Mount, Jesus tells us to "seek first" God's kingdom and His righteousness (Matt. 6:33). We are to give priority to that seeking. Jesus is again stressing intensity; one who yearns for righteousness will seek it.

Paul also speaks of intensity in our yearning for righteousness. Twice he told Timothy to "pursue" righteousness (1 Tim. 6:11; 2 Tim. 2:22; the Greek word for "pursue" is a different word from the word "seek" in Matt. 6:33). In short, the Bible says that we are to desire, seek, and pursue righteousness. Our seeking and pursuing has passion attached to it.

To desire, seek, and pursue righteousness is to align our desires and our activities with those of Christ, our righteousness (1 Cor. 1:30). Jesus expressed His spiritual hunger when He said, "My *food* is to do the will of Him who sent Me, and to accomplish His work" (John 4:34, emphasis added). We align our heart and our desires with His, because being like Him is our goal.

The Common Thread of Need

Through these first four beatitudes runs a common thread of need. God loves the needy: the widows, the orphans, the prisoners, the strangers in the land. Need is the key to God's heart. God supplies according to the spiritual need we express to Him. And it is a blessing to have the right need.

The poor in spirit need God. The spiritual life starts there, in repentance. It continues there as we increasingly know our need of God.

Mourners need the Holy Spirit. Although they are broken, they are able to avoid resentment because they rely on the Spirit of God for their comfort and instruction. Hostility and bitterness have no place in their heart. They turned to the proper source to supply their need, and their need leads to blessing.

The meek need God, but they also need others. This quality eliminates the spirit of independence. The body of Christ begins its real cohesion when its members recognize their need for one another.

Those hungering and thirsting need spiritual food (John 4:34). They need the milk of the word (1 Pet. 2:2) as well as solid food (Heb. 5:14). Above all, they need Christ in His fullness. He *is* our righteousness. This desperate yearning marks the climax of our progression of need.

God's intention is that circumstances highlight the spiritual nature of our real needs. The mind of Christ is to seek spiritual illumination when our circumstances may appear to be adverse. God's supply in our spiritual need leads to spiritual growth.

The Second Four Beatitudes: Our Becoming Like Christ

With the fifth beatitude, "Blessed are the merciful," the element of need suddenly disappears. Like the first four, the second four beatitudes are closely related to one another, they differ in kind from the first four. In them, we are in an atmosphere of projecting the image of Christ to the world positively. Christ is merciful, pure, peacemaking, and persecuted.

The Merciful

Jesus began this group of outwardly Christlike qualities by saying, "Blessed are the merciful, for they shall receive mercy." Giving mercy is the appropriate starting place for showing the mind of Christ to others. In showing mercy, we are meeting a need that others have.

The Lord said that the merciful would obtain mercy. Back of this blessing is the principle of reciprocity. God will give back to us what we give others. He helps us be what we are determined to be.

David said in his prayer after deliverance from his enemies, "With the kind [KJV: merciful] Thou dost show Thyself kind [KJV: merciful], With the blameless Thou dost show Thyself blameless; With the pure Thou dost show Thyself pure, And with the perverted Thou dost show Thyself astute" (2 Sam. 22:26–27).

During Pharaoh's plagues, we are told repeatedly that his heart was hardened. In the second and fourth plagues (frogs and insects), the Bible specifically says that Pharaoh hardened his heart (Exod. 8:15, 32). At that point, the action came from Pharaoh's will. In the sixth plague (boils), the wording changes: "And *the* LORD hardened Pharaoh's heart" (Exod. 9:12, emphasis added; God had said He would do this as early as Exod. 7:3). God helped Pharaoh be what he was determined to be. God reciprocated.

How like Christ is the grand quality of mercy! The Gospels mention His compassion on five different occasions (Matt. 9:36, 14:14; Mark 1:41, 8:2; Luke 7:13). He was also merciful in forgiving sins (Matt. 9:2; Luke 7:48). Through Jesus, we learn what the mercy of God is. It is having compassion and forgiving those who wrong us.

The Pure in Heart

The second beatitude in this second group is, "Blessed are the pure in heart, for they shall see God." The principle here is giving one's heart wholly to God. If our hearts are given wholly to God, we will not allow foreign elements to enter. Our hearts will be pure. The Bible says that

David's heart was "wholly devoted to the LORD his God" (1 Kings 11:4; an NASB note says that the literal meaning of the Hebrew is that his heart was "complete" with God).

Attributing a "wholly devoted heart" to David bewildered me since he committed both adultery and murder. Then I realized what a man of song David was. When he was a shepherd boy, he was singing to God. When he was rich and a king, he sang songs to God. If he was running from his enemies, he had a song. After his mighty victories, he attributed his victories to God in song. David indeed sinned, but in his sin he wrote the most heartbroken hymn of repentance in the Bible, Psalm 51.

David always had a song. Perpetual song can only come from the heart. David's performance was shameful, but his heart was praiseworthy. His song shows the condition of his heart. None of us will give the Lord a perfect performance. Our performance will not be "pure." But God does not expect that from us. He wants us instead to give Him our heart (Prov. 23:26).

Webster's dictionary says that the heart in this meaning is "the whole personality, including intellectual as well as emotional functions or traits." The heart in this sense permeates our language. It can be broken. We can be heartsick. We speak of persons as being big-hearted or having no heart. All these expressions involve the whole personality. The Bible is telling us to give all of ourselves to the Lord.

Asa's heart was also given to the Lord. His performance was poor, like David's, but his heart "was wholly devoted to the LORD all his days" (1 Kings 15:14). God is more interested in our heart than our performance.

If we are pure in heart, our hearts will have no extraneous loyalty. It is the heart that is unmixed. Our devotion to our family and friends will derive from our love for God. If it does not, we are in danger of loving family or friends more than God. If we reserve a part of our heart for some earthly affection that separates us from God or takes precedence over God, we are not pure. All the loves of our life are related to and spring from our love for God.

Being pure in heart does not require a perfect performance. Rather it requires our giving our whole selves to the Lord. God is jealous (Exod. 20:5). He is looking for abandoned self-giving.

The mind of Christ is to be pure in heart. Jesus said, "I am not of this world" (John 8:23). He was totally given to His Father from His earliest known utterance (Luke 2:49) to His last discourse (John 17:4). We cannot duplicate Christ's performance, but we can have His heart.

The Peacemakers

Jesus next blessed those who brought harmony into the world: "Blessed are the peacemakers, for they shall be called sons of God." Our principle here is reconciliation. God wants to see unity with Himself and unity within the body of Christ.

Obtaining unity means seeking reconciliation. The reconcilers will be called sons of God. In reconciling, we are like Jesus and have a family resemblance.

Some of us resist reconciliation because we fear compromise. Compromise is, in fact, a danger (see chapter 4). We cannot compromise doctrine, but some of our fears are really fears of compromising culture. Christ is acultural. His message has found root in radically diverse cultures. We tend to become more attached to our culture than to our doctrines. By *culture* I mean the way we do things in our Christian life or the way we have church.

Without compromising doctrine, I have found it possible to worship and fellowship with many different expressions of the Christian faith. In fact, I have learned much from certain cultures that are radically different from the one in which I grew up. I have taught "The Mind of Christ" several times to multidenominational and multiracial groups with excellent responses from all denominations and races. I have even taught it to denominations and church groups that had doctrines or practiced polity radically different from my own. Yet we enjoyed a blessed fellowship in our common loyalty to Christ.

The key to crossing cultures is to maintain the centrality of Christ. So long as His deity, His humanity, His works, and His basic instruction for living are not altered or compromised, we can rally around His person. In effect, in our multicultural meetings we found peace with one another through our common loyalty to and submission to Christ.

This reconciliation, I believe, is the mind of Christ. He prayed for it (John 17:21, 23). We need not compromise our doctrine to love our brothers or sisters, whoever they are. Jesus reconciled. "For He Himself is our peace, who made both groups [Jew and Gentile] into one, and broke down the barrier of the dividing wall, by abolishing in His flesh the enmity . . . that in Himself He might make the two into one new man, thus establishing peace, and might reconcile them both in one body to God through the cross, by it having put to death the enmity. And He came and preached peace to you who were far away, and peace to those who were near; for through Him we both have our access in one Spirit to the Father" (Eph. 2:14–18).

Those Who Have Been Persecuted

Jesus concluded this group of blessings by saying, "Blessed are those who have been persecuted for the sake of righteousness, for theirs is the kingdom of heaven." He added an extra blessing for the persecuted: "Blessed are you when men cast insults at you, and persecute you, and say all kinds of evil against you falsely, on account of Me" (Matt. 5:11). Note that this last verse has no consequent phrase like the preceding: "for theirs is the kingdom of heaven." It was not intended to be a ninth beatitude, but an amplification of the eighth.

The principle behind these statements is the principle of identification with Christ. All of the beatitudes lead up to this principle. The primary object of this book is to help you in the lifelong process of conforming to His image, whatever that may entail.

Persecution should be expected. Jesus said, "A slave is not greater than his master. If they persecuted Me, they will also persecute you; if they kept My word, they will keep yours also" (John 15:20). People will treat us as they treated Jesus.

How many people would accept Christ if they knew that it would bring difficulties? Paul did, for he had been afflicting Christians with severe punishment. He knew the mind-set of the persecutors. Later he would say, "I count all things to be loss in view of the surpassing value of knowing Christ Jesus my Lord, for whom I have suffered the loss of all things, and count them but rubbish in order that I may gain Christ" (Phil. 3:8). The universal witness of martyrs and others who have suffered for their faith is knowing that Christ is worth the cost.

The first-century church knew and accepted this fact. For Stephen and James, knowing Christ was worth their lives. For Peter it was worth being jailed. For John it was worth exile. Down through the centuries, countless martyrs have endured torture or death for the sake of Christ.

A second reason for enduring these trials is the eternal reward after the suffering is over. The Bible tells us, "If we suffer, we shall also reign with him" (2 Tim. 2:12 KJV). As Paul finished his earthly work (and it involved much persecution), he declared, "I have fought the good fight, I have finished the course, I have kept the faith; in the future there is laid up for me the crown of righteousness, which the Lord, the righteous Judge, will award me on that day; and not only to me, but also to all who have loved His appearing" (2 Tim. 4:7).

Above all, we endure trial because we love Christ. He loved us first and gave His life for us (Gal. 2:20). For us awaits "things which eye has not seen and ear has not heard, and which have not entered the heart of man, all that God has prepared for those who love Him" (1 Cor. 2:9).

The Common Thread of Giving

Through the second group of four blessings also runs a common thread. The first four in their profound need were receivers. They received God, His Holy Spirit, others, and spiritual food. The common thread among the second four is that of giving.

God also loves the givers. He is the greatest of all givers. He gave the supreme gift, His only begotten Son (John 3:16). He gives salvation (Eph. 2:8). All perfect gifts are from Him (James 1:17). Jesus tells us, "It is more blessed to give than to receive" (Acts 20:35).

Those who show mercy are giving grace to the world. Grace is the umbrella of God's unmerited favor toward us, and mercy is our action under that umbrella. It shows God's compassion to the world. More importantly (and with more difficulty), it shows God's forgiveness toward those who offend us. The mind of Christ is to forgive enemies.

Those who are pure in heart are giving holiness to the world and especially to the church. Holiness is glorious (Exod. 15:11 KJV), and some people will be drawn to the Lord if our example is pure and holy. Real holiness might repel some persons also. Holiness of life helps define the issue of authentic Christianity.

The peacemakers impart the calming gift of security. They also give wholeness.[1] Parties at war are in a precarious position. The reconcilers bring harmony to broken relationships. Doing that is like God, it is the mind of Christ.

The persecuted give all; they give self. This is the highest gift we can give the world—a faithful witness through suffering for Christ. The martyrs are our greatest teachers. Those who suffer for their faith provide the world with the knowledge of the supreme value of Christ.

The Symmetry of God's Work in Our Lives

The beatitudes show us the way God works in our lives. The first four turn our minds to God. In poverty of spirit, we fear God. In brokenness, we learn from the Holy Comforter. In meekness, we learn our position before God and in the body of Christ. In hunger and thirst, we come to depend on God to supply our deepest needs.

The second four beatitudes turn our minds to others. We show mercy to other people, not to God. In purity of heart, we show others holiness. We make peace between others; God does not need our peace. Who will persecute you? Others! God does not do that.

By dealing with us in these ways, God turns our attention first to Him, and then to our fellow man. This order follows the sequence of the two greatest commandments. Jesus said, "The foremost [commandment] is, 'Hear, O Israel! The Lord our God is one Lord; and you shall love the Lord your God with all your heart, and with all your soul, and with all your mind, and with all your strength.' The second is this, 'You shall love your neighbor as yourself'" (Mark 12:29–31).

In the first four beatitudes, God is using circumstances to bring us to the point of need. In the second group, we use circumstances to bring others to Christ or to help them know Him more thoroughly. The first four are necessary for our learning of God. The second four are necessary for our demonstration of Christ. We must learn about God before we can show Him to the world.

God's basic work in the first four is an inner work. It is silent and secret. It results in a healthy fear of the Lord, ascribing to Him His glory and magnifying Him instead of self. God's basic work in the second four is an outer work. Through us, God demonstrates His mercy, purity, and peace to the world. The inner harmonizes with the outer. Once again, God is leading us into a higher integration of mind.

The first four are the door to greatness in God's kingdom. To arrive at Christian nobility, we must begin by knowing God. The second four are the practice of greatness. Greatness forgives and will show mercy. It is holy and knows how to bring peace. It is capable of any sacrifice God may require.

God is working in all eight of the Beatitudes, but He works differently in the two groups. The first four are the keys to God's heart. There we learn of God. The second four are the keys to expressing Christ.

Practical Application

God wants you to be noble. His method of training you for this nobility may be more rigorous than you would have chosen. Below are a set of attitudes that indicate majesty and nobility from heaven's standpoint. Some of these attitudes are learned only in the crucible of suffering. Pray about each statement in relation to your own life. Ask God to help you become noble.

Poor in spirit	1. I am sensitive to the enormous gulf that separates my creaturely nature from God's divine nature.
	2. I can do nothing without God.
	3. I do not resent God's showing me my shortcomings.
Those who mourn	4. When life gets hard, I turn immediately to the help of the Holy Spirit.
	5. Past breakings have purified me.
	6. I have no bitterness toward God for my past misfortunes.
	7. I will harbor no bitterness over the rigorous training of nobility as God molds me and shapes me.
The meek	8. My eyes are fastened upward on God.
	9. I need others in the body of Christ.
	10. The good of the body of Christ is more important to me than my position in it.
Those who hunger and thirst	11. Righteousness is more important to me than food.
	12. I thank God whenever I learn something about Him or acquire a new spiritual insight.
	13. The character of Jesus controls me more and more.
The merciful	14. I am a compassionate person.
	15. I consistently respond to other persons in need.
	16. I forgive from the heart persons who wrong me.
The pure in heart	17. I harbor no secret sin.
	18. Whenever I sin, it grieves me.
	19. Today I give God my heart.
	20. I love God more than any person on earth.
The peacemakers	21. I am reconciled to God and to my fellow man.
	22. My first reaction when I perceive differences among others is to seek reconciliation.
	23. I exalt the person of Christ above my own culture.
The persecuted	24. I have experienced difficulty because Christ is Lord of my life.
	25. My loyalty to Christ is the greatest loyalty I have.
	26. I am certain that I will remain loyal to Christ no matter how that loyalty is tested.

Conclusion

Christ's humanity, expressed in the beatitudes, facilitates in me the mental quality of authority. God's goal for me is royal princeliness. My growth can only be measured by Christ's nobility of spirit. He enables my perfect humanity in His role as Brother. He transforms me.

c h a p t e r   e i g h t

Humble and Obedient

he humbled himself, and became obedient unto death

While I was writing the book *The Disciple's Prayer Life,* I asked several friends to read the manuscript. I was especially concerned that the chapter on worship communicate well. The first person I shared this chapter with brought it back to me and said, "I'm sorry, but I don't understand what you are saying."

I was chagrined, but I immediately started over. I failed again. In fact, I don't know how many drafts of that chapter I made as I tried to discover what would communicate effectively.

Finally, I realized in prayer that my approach had unconsciously been that of an "expert" on worship. At that point, my ideas were more important than communication. I decided to change my approach completely and my way of praying. I was a servant to the Lord, seeking to communicate His ideas so that they would be understood. I was also a servant to my readers, and my job was to speak in a way that they would seize these ideas and apply them to their lives.

The most important change was my way of praying. Normally, I address God as Father, but often I use other titles to indicate a relationship with Him. Now I prayed, "Master, I don't know how to do this. But You are the Master and I am the servant. As Master, You know the precise needs of my work. I depend on You. As Your servant, I ask You to show me exactly what will communicate."

This approach was what God had been waiting for me to discover. The "expert" didn't know what God wanted, but the servant was in a position to hear from the Lord. Almost immediately I was alive with inspiration. After my next draft of the worship chapter, every person who read it responded favorably. In a "superior" position, I was unable to follow the leadership of the Lord. In a "lowly" position, I heard very clearly.

It seems strange to devote an entire chapter to humility and obedience, but humility is the main point of the hymn in Philippians 2:5–11. In the preceding four verses, Paul had made a plea for lowliness, and he reinforces this specific point by quoting the hymn on which this book is based.

Here again, Christ is our example. The incarnation itself is an act of humility (Heb. 2:16). God had to stoop low to become a man. Everything about His earthly life was lowly. He was born in a stable, and His cradle was a feeding trough.

The circumstances of His life were modest and unassuming. He grew up in a village despised by the people of His day (John 1:46). Had we been writing the script for His story, we would have placed Him in the Jewish capital, Jerusalem, under the best-known teachers of the day. Paul, unlike Christ, was highly credentialed. Yet he said, "For you know the grace of our Lord Jesus Christ, that though He was rich, yet for your sake He became poor" (2 Cor. 8:9). He submitted to His parents and lived in obscurity for thirty years. Try to fathom the enormous significance of this fact: God incarnate anonymously walked the streets of an obscure little town for most of His earthly life. He worked as a carpenter and served the needs of the common rural districts around Nazareth.

Incredibly, He who was perfectly holy submitted to a baptism intended for sinners. One of His purposes was to identify with the lowest and vilest of us. John the Baptist, with keen perception, "tried to prevent Him, saying, 'I have need to be baptized by You, and You come to me?'" (Matt. 3:14).

Jesus Christ submitted to His own creation. By virtue of His nature and office, He was inherently higher than the high priest, higher than the governor, higher than Caesar. He was above all humans and human agencies. Yet He gave Himself to the service of others. He expressly said, "For even the Son of Man did not come to be served, but to serve, and to give His life a ransom for many" (Mark 10:45).

The supreme example of humility throughout all history is Jesus' willing submission to the ignoble death of a criminal. People today can hardly comprehend the contempt in which the Roman cross was held during the first century. Modern execution is relatively humane and often enlists the sympathy of large numbers of people. Roman crucifixion, even more than Egyptian or Syrian crucifixion, was considered shameful beyond anything known in our times. Roman citizens were exempt from crucifixion. Only the lowest criminals and slaves were crucified. In the Lord's Supper the night before He died, Jesus said to His disciples, "For I tell you, that this which is written must be fulfilled in Me, 'And He was numbered with transgressors'; for that which refers to Me has its fulfillment" (Luke 22:37, quoting Isa. 53:12).

No other person ever stooped so low as Jesus did. His original position was absolute in its exaltation. As the second person of the Trinity, He occupied the highest possible position and rank. Yet He came to the lowest village, in the lowest peasant rank, traveled simply as an itinerant preacher, gave His life in lowly service, and died the most despised death possible in His time. He is our example!

Pride and Humility

Most of us are repulsed by arrogance and haughtiness. Prideful people are not attractive. Yet strangely we are not attracted to the opposite, lowliness and humility, at least not as a quality for ourselves. We do not seek out the servants and the insignificant. Even though pride is repulsive, we seek out the important. Perhaps even that is selfish. We derive a feeling of importance from being with important people.

If we find pride repugnant, how much more would God be repulsed by it? From the vantage point of His exalted station, the slightest presumption is a breach in the noble courtesy of dealing with divinity. God says, "I will also put an end to the arrogance of the proud, And abase the haughtiness of the ruthless" (Isa. 13:11).

The humble fear the Lord. That is a part of being humble. The humble look up. They cannot look down on others, for they consider themselves to be at the bottom. The proud disregard the Lord, for their look is always downward.

Humble people are open to the Lord and to others. This also is a part of the meaning of being humble. God often chooses to speak through others. Jesus always listened to other people. He was especially sensitive to those in need. He heard Bartimaeus when others were silencing him (Mark 10:46–49). All the good listeners I have known have been humble people. Proud people are closed to others; all their attention is on self.

Humble people exalt others. They are primarily other-directed, first upward to God and then outwardly to others. This, by the way, is basic to mental health. The mind of Christ is a robust, active, and healthy mind. Proud people are inwardly directed, and this is dangerous to mental health. The scribes aggrandized self. Jesus warned His followers, "Beware of the scribes, who like to walk around in long robes, and love respectful greetings in the market places, and chief seats in the synagogues, and places of honor at banquets, . . . and for appearance's sake offer long prayers; these will receive greater condemnation" (Luke 20:46–47).

Parenthetically, we should note that false humility is unhealthy. By false humility I mean a self-degrading attitude that does not see God's greatness as the primary basis for our humility. This false attitude is full of self-pity. False humility may degrade self in front of others, but it also whines and complains at its lot in life.

I have known people who incessantly reminded family and friends of their self-sacrifice. Sometimes this doing without ended by costing others extra effort to accommodate the "humility" of the person. People like that are really self-centered. Their humility is false.

True humility does indeed sacrifice itself, but it never costs others. Real humility is an attitude and act of the will (as is false humility). Genuine humility grows out of a faith in the greatness of God and a confidence that God will act. It is a life of faith and rests in the finished accomplishments of Christ.

True humility is able to love because it is genuinely other-directed. "Love does not brag and is not arrogant" (1 Cor. 13:4). Conceited people love only themselves. If anyone has ever known love in a mature sense, he or she knows that love is humble. Love wants to serve the object of its affection, and we cannot serve without humility.

Pride, on the other hand, scorns others. Goliath was proud. "When the Philistine looked and saw David, he disdained him" (1 Sam. 17:42). His pride led to his downfall. He was so self-centered that he could only perceive one kind of strength—his own. David's confidence was in the Lord, not in himself. Humility's strength is in the Lord. That is a strength that may shock people when they perceive its power. It killed Goliath.

Humble people want to encourage others. They enjoy seeing others blossom. This also is healthy for the mind. Proud people discourage others. Their stance is to threaten.

Humble people enjoy seeing other people succeed. They are generous, and generosity is one mark of greatness. Generosity also makes for good mental health, for it provides more occasions of joy as God blesses others. Proud people only rejoice when they themselves succeed. The occasions for joy are penalized when we cannot rejoice in the success of others.

Humility's obedience depends on the initiative of God. Since God dwells with the humble (Isa. 57:15), they are in constant contact with Him. They know when He speaks and are quick to obey Him. If God chooses to delay, waiting is not difficult for them. Proud people want to obey only their self-exalting impulses. They cannot hear God, for "God is opposed to the proud" (James 4:6). The humble work on God's initiative; the proud work on their own initiative.

Humble people are able to make peace. They are reconcilers. Peace may require yielding, and the humble will yield. Proud people create strife. Self-centeredness will not submit to another. "Through presumption comes nothing but strife, But with those who receive counsel is wisdom" (Prov. 13:10).

Since humility produces peace, it leads to unity among Christians. Paul said, "I therefore, the prisoner of the Lord, entreat you to walk in a manner worthy of the calling with which you have been called, with all humility and gentleness, with patience, showing forbearance to one another in love, being diligent to preserve the unity of the Spirit in the bond of peace" (Eph. 4:1–3). Christ's prayer for unity was one of his strongest recorded prayers. The Christian who values Christ highly will seek to honor His desire for unity.

Unity requires bonding. Bonding requires submitting to others—to their desires, their personality, and perhaps even their culture. God will honor that act of lowliness. Bonding requires emphasizing that which we have in common. The one factor that all Christians have in common is Christ Himself. If we really emphasized the person of Christ, it would take a lifetime to exhaust our commonalities in Him.

Humility sees the value of the larger group, or the church, or the body. Pride sees only the individual. Instead of cohesion, it seeks prominence. Pride fragments the body of Christ.

The humble perceive divine revelation. Their openness makes revelation possible. After the seventy returned from their mission, Christ prayed, "I praise Thee, O Father, Lord of heaven and earth, that Thou didst hide these things from the wise and intelligent and didst reveal them to babes" (Luke 10:21). The prideful concentrate on self.

With all this in mind, it is small wonder that the Bible says, "With the humble is wisdom" (Prov. 11:2). Humility leads to openness, love, encouragement, obedience, peace, unity, and revelation.

Pride is foolish. An arrogant Pharaoh demanded, "Who is the LORD that I should obey His voice to let Israel go?" (Exod. 5:2). His army was later virtually destroyed. A conceited Haman conceived the idea of killing all of Mordecai's people when Mordecai would not bow to him. He ended by leading Mordecai through the streets as he proclaimed Mordecai's honor (Esther 6:11–12). In our day too, pride leads to our downfall.

The Best-Kept Secret

It is strange that some of us give lip service to the lordship of Christ, but in practice we ignore His teachings. Most mature Christians are familiar with such words as "Blessed are the poor in spirit" or "Blessed are they that mourn." Yet we tend to be bitter and recriminating when God speaks to us through adversity.

Jesus' teaching on humility is among the best known of His teachings, and yet the power and nobility of humility remains the best-kept secret in the Christian world. As the disciples approached Capernaum, they argued about which of them would be the greatest. Christ used their argument as an occasion to clarify the true nature of spiritual greatness. "And sitting down, He called the twelve and said to them, 'If anyone wants to be first, he shall be last of all, and servant of all'" (Mark 9:35).

In the world, the pinnacle of success is often reached by ambition and greediness. Many people try to operate within the kingdom by grasping and self-exaltation. Tragically, some succeed in this way. We get what we aim for.

This is why Christians should not judge other Christians. We have no way of knowing exactly how God evaluates us. It is possible that, finally, under God we will see some seemingly successful Christians as pygmies. The opposite is also true. We will see some very humble people in the phenomenal stature that is really theirs when we see through God's eyes.

According to Jesus, the way up is down. Real nobility is not in position, but in character. God never prizes the position we reach, but the character we attain. For this reason, when we finally perceive Christ's world-view, we will be shocked to see that the last really are first and the least are valued for their greatness.

One of the most electrifying statements Jesus made was His declaration that greatness consisted in childlikeness (Matt. 18:4). The world does not always value children, but God does (Matt. 18:5–6). Likewise, the world does not value humility, but, as we have seen, God does. Children are open and responsive and therefore are learners. Learning is simple for a child, but for an adult it is an act of the will.

At the end of Jesus' life, the disciples once again argued about their relative importance (they did this three times). This time Jesus made His strongest statement about relative stature in His kingdom: "The kings of the Gentiles lord it over them; and those who have authority over them are called 'Benefactors.' But not so with you, but let him who is greatest among you become as the youngest, and the leader as the servant" (Luke 22:25–26).

Suppose that right now we could see a world in which Jesus' principles were practiced literally. Position would depend on character. Even ability or I.Q. would not really matter in attaining recognition—only character. That manner of thinking is almost not feasible from the standpoint of our present world-view.

Aspects of character that are rarely noticed now would become important to us—such as purity, guilelessness, honesty, simplicity, deference, and service. People with those qualities are the ones most likely to fail in our present world system. Therefore, many Christians deliberately avoid cultivating these biblical traits. Yet they are the qualities Jesus wanted them to have. Jesus rarely paid a compliment. One of these few occasions happened when He praised Nathanael's guilelessness (John 1:47).

Small wonder that the disciples failed to comprehend. Jesus was presenting them with a world-view precisely opposite from the one in which they lived. It is characteristic of this world, not merely of our time. We still misunderstand. God's high opinion of lowliness and humility remains the best-kept secret in Christendom.

These lessons can be applied practically. The attitude of humility can be adopted as an act of the will. James 4:10 places it in the form of an imperative verb: "Humble yourselves in the presence of the Lord, and He will exalt you." We can achieve what the Bible commands.

We must require of ourselves that we become other-directed. That is a matter of attention, and we have control over our attention. Much of having the mind of Christ is an act of the will, yet it is not self-effort. It is directing our attention to the leadership of the Holy Spirit.

The first great other to which we direct our attention is God. The most appropriate place to begin doing that is in prayer. Each morning when I prepare to pray, I begin by kneeling. The act of kneeling is a conscious indication of submitting. Then before anything else, I spend several minutes meditating on the attributes of God—omniscience, omnipotence, omnipresence, absolute holiness, and such. I want to be sure my heart senses fear and reverence before I proceed. Any Christian can perform this deliberate act of submission. It also puts my prayer requests into the context of holiness and power.

Sometimes I feel such reverence that I need also to spend some time concentrating on the person of God in order to have courage in the presence of His absolutes. He is also Father, Master, Brother (one of the names of Christ), and Bridegroom. Although His holiness seems to separate Him into "the high and holy place," He is our Father and our Friend. He wants to hear from us. Our job is to maintain the proper perspective.

Once we have God in perspective, we can easily remember that orientation as we relate to Him in Bible study, meditation, witness, and ministry. He is Creator, and we are creatures, albeit ultimately the highest of His creation.

We must also apply our other-directedness to our fellow man. Paul admonished, "Do not be haughty in mind, but associate with the lowly" (Rom. 12:16). Christ did that. He chose for His friends the poor of the land. He associated with those who were outcasts and despised. At the same time He did not disdain the Capernaum nobleman or the Roman centurion. He reserved His disdain for the haughty and the sophisticated.

It is far too easy for us to stratify the various societies in which we move. We are rich and poor, strong and weak, intelligent and stupid, sophisticated and naive, powerful and weak, or elite and lowly. Christ did not stratify the ordinary communities of the people of His day except for the haughty ones, whom He censured.

God sees all of us from His high and holy standpoint, far above the richest or most intelligent of us. From that standpoint, He sees little difference in the great and the small, whatever the dimension or measure might be.

We are to adopt that viewpoint. This does not mean that we are divine, but it does mean that we are noble. Haughtiness is petty. From

God's exalted viewpoint, it is foolish. God's outlook is the most intelligent stance we can take.

Our job is to extend the grace of God to others, whoever they may be. We love them, not because they are lovable, but because we are Christians. Out of this love, we minister to them. We show them what God is like. That is what Christ did.

Radical Obedience

We saw in chapter 6 that servants obey. The emphasis there was on alertness to the voice of the master. Now, as we go deeper into our hymn, we learn the extent of real obedience.

"He became obedient unto death." The obedience of Christ was the most radical obedience in the history of God's people. Although many martyrs have paid the price for obedience with their lives, none of them paid the radical price of bearing the sin of the world. "Christ redeemed us from the curse of the Law, having become a curse for us" (Gal. 3:13).

Jesus' sole purpose in life was to do the will of His Father (John 6:38; Heb. 10:9). He declared, "I have not even come on My own initiative, but He sent Me" (John 8:42). He consulted His Father in every act (John 5:19, 30). His final act of submission was difficult, even for Him, but His obedience was absolute.

With God only one kind of obedience counts, and that is total obedience. Our goals are His goals. He will not give us a command that we are unable to perform. Jesus told us, "Not everyone who says to Me, 'Lord, Lord,' will enter the kingdom of heaven; but he who does the will of My Father who is in heaven" (Matt. 7:21).

God's first call to all of us is to full-time living for Christ. For a part of my life, I served the Lord in a secular vocation. However, since 1959, I have felt my call to be to live for Christ in whatever way my vocation would provide the opportunity. The mind of Christ for most Christians is to make their living in a secular job, but to live for Christ in that job and in their lives so that their secular job will end up counting for Christ's kingdom in some significant way. Radical obedience is possible for every believer, regardless of the particular work they are doing. How is your life counting for Christ through radical obedience?

Many other believers are called to missionary service, or to any one of the various types of ministry available to us in our day. When Christians fail to respond to this calling of God, they leave important holes in the kingdom work. The Father had a plan for Christ before Christ entered the world. He has a plan for us prior to our entering the world (Eph. 2:10).

Many are not hearing about Christ because someone has failed to respond to the long-term plan. That may be as a clerk or as a bank president. It may be as a preacher or a missionary. All of us are called to live for Christ 100 percent of our lives. Have you heard the voice of God calling you to live fully for Him, regardless of your particular vocation? The mind of Christ draws no limits.

Conclusion

Christ's self-emptying is the supreme example of humility. To have the mind of Christ, we must deliberately humble ourselves by becoming other-directed, first to God and then to others. We are in a position to build the kingdom when we humble ourselves. Because of Christ's humility, He was able to obey radically. If I am humble, I can obey in the same way Christ did. He enables my humility in His office as the Righteous Servant. His example is my goal.

chapter nine

Crucified

even death on the cross

A s He entered the Gethsemane ordeal, Jesus told Peter, James, and John, "My soul is deeply grieved to the point of death; remain here and keep watch" (Mark 14:34).[1] This is the only time Jesus ever asked for help. The strange prayers of Gethsemane are so different from any other prayer He ever prayed that it seems almost incredible to hear Jesus say, "Abba! Father! All things are possible for Thee; remove this cup from Me; yet not what I will, but what Thou wilt" (v. 36).

When we are in trauma, the capillaries in the sweat glands just under the surface of the skin dilate. You see this when people blush. If the stress is intense enough, the blood vessels pressing against the sweat glands burst. The blood has nowhere to go except out through the sweat glands, and the person sweats blood. This rare phenomenon has been observed by modern doctors. The medical name for this is hematidrosis.

Whenever hematidrosis occurs, the skin is so sensitized that the slightest touch is painful. As the skin oozes blood, the skin becomes fragile and tender.[2] The process of sweating blood also produces marked weakness and possible shock.[3] Although Jesus' body was robust from three years of extensive walking from the extreme north to the south of Israel, His body now entered the long ordeal of the trials and physical abuse weakened, already sensitized to pain and highly susceptible to the ghastly rigors ahead of Him.

The betrayal of Judas was important to the priests because of two factors. First, as a disciple, he knew the secret whereabouts of Jesus. The priests wanted Jesus arrested, convicted, and on the cross before His large following could rebel. They preferred the advantage of an arrest late at night so they could rush through the trials. Their conspiracy needed to be consummated before the Sabbath began, because the ensuing week of the Feast of Unleavened Bread would preclude any other action until the feast was over.

Second, Judas would be the chief witness. Hebrew law at the time did not have a prosecuting attorney. The witnesses themselves served as accusers, that is, in effect as prosecutors.[4] Judas's betrayal, therefore, technically was an offer to prosecute Jesus. The law concerning admissible witnesses and evidence was fair and offered a problem to the priests in securing a valid conviction.[5] The priests knew that they dare not miss this opportunity for a reliable witness for their case. Judas took a large party to the scene (John 18:3).[6]

The Three Religious Trials

The Trial Before Annas

Jesus was taken first, not to the house of the reigning high priest, but to Annas, the wicked old political boss of Jerusalem who had controlled the priesthood for so many years. Significantly at this point, no witnesses were introduced.

Annas asked Jesus two questions. First, he asked about Jesus' disciples. Obviously he had reason to suspect that Jesus had secret disciples in high offices; Annas had no concern for Galilean fishermen or tax collectors. The disciples might betray Jesus, they might deny Him, but He would never betray His own. Jesus simply ignored the question.

Annas next asked Jesus what He taught—a question so absurd that it is incredible that Annas even asked. Two days prior to this night, the priests had spent the day unsuccessfully trying to trap Jesus with questions as He was teaching (Luke 20:1–40). To point out the hypocrisy of the question, Jesus stated the obvious truth, "I have spoken openly to the world; I always taught in synagogues, and in the temple, where all the Jews come together; and I spoke nothing in secret. Why do you question Me? Question those who have heard what I spoke to them [an allusion to the priests present on every side of Him]; behold, these know what I said" (John 18:20–21). When He said this, an official struck Him in the face—a face powerfully sensitized by hematidrosis. This blow brought the first of many contusions to His body.

The Trial Before Caiaphas

Jesus was next taken to the house of the reigning high priest, Caiaphas, Annas's son-in-law. This was during the very late hours of the night.[7] Here a committee of the Sanhedrin had convened to try Jesus. They probably were a small unit composed of close friends of the high priest.[8]

However, a new and embarrassing situation developed at this point. The chief witness, Judas, had disappeared.[9] Caught without the expected witness, the priests had to produce other witnesses quickly. They were obviously unprepared for this, and the witnesses were also unprepared. Their testimony did not agree, as required by law.[10]

One witness misquoted Jesus. On His first casting out of the money-changers, the priests had demanded that He cite His authority for doing so. At that time, Jesus had told them, "Destroy this temple, and in three days I will *raise* [*egeiro*] it up" (John 2:19, emphasis added). The false witness stated that Jesus said that He would build (*oikodomeo*) another temple (Mark 14:58). The word *raise*, which Jesus used, is used twenty-seven times later in the New Testament of the resurrection of His physical body; Jesus clearly referred to His resurrection. Mark, however, tells us, "And not even in this respect was their testimony consistent" (14:59).

The prosecution was stymied. The flustered Caiaphas demanded, "Do You make no answer? What is it that these men are testifying against You?" (v. 60). Since no charge had been validated by the necessary plurality of witnesses, Jesus needed no defense. He stood in His regal silence, waiting for the prosecution's next move.

Frustrated, Caiaphas finally got to the main point. The heart of the leadership's anger with Christ is shown in the fact that they did not bring up the many charges of Sabbath violations with which they had plagued Jesus for so many months. They even failed to pursue the flimsy charge of His claim to rebuild a destroyed temple. Instead, Caiaphas demonstrated their own intense concern over the person of Jesus by resorting to the Oath of Testimony that required a truthful answer,[11] "I adjure You by the living God, that You tell us whether You are the Christ, the Son of God" (Matt. 26:63).

At long last, Jesus had legitimate reason to answer, although the accused could not legally be compelled to testify against himself.[12] He told Caiaphas and the court, "I am. You have said it yourself" (Mark 14:62 and Matt. 26:64 combined). From their point of view, this supplied them with the information necessary to bring a charge of blasphemy. To make sure that the priests could not mistake His intentions, Jesus now quoted two famous Messianic prophecies, Psalm 110:1 and Daniel 7:13: "Nevertheless I tell you, hereafter you shall see the Son of Man sitting at the right hand of power, and coming on the clouds of heaven" (Matt. 26:64).

Legally the high priest could not tear his clothes (Lev. 21:10), but Caiaphas now dramatically tore his robe the length of his hand, the length prescribed by tradition when blasphemy was committed.[13] He proclaimed, "He has blasphemed!" (Matt. 26:65). They were now relieved of the annoying problem of legitimate witnesses, and Caiaphas declared, "What further need do we have of witnesses? Behold, you have now heard the blasphemy; what do you think?" (vv. 65–66). The committee cried, apparently in unison, "He is deserving of death!" (v. 66), and they condemned Him to death, even though the "court" was in a private home in the middle of the night.

They had not known what Jesus might do when arrested. They had heard of the prisoner's amazing miracles and mysterious powers. But now they had had Him in their power for hours, and He had performed no mighty works on His own behalf. They certainly knew of the intense loyalty of His followers, but His disciples had run away.

The priests became drunk with power. They blindfolded Jesus and began a horrendous series of tortures. They spit on Him. While they struck Him with their fists, they would sneer, "Prophesy to us, You Christ; who is the one who hit You?" (Matt. 26:68; it seems likely that the priests had guards administer the physical aspects of the punishment). Luke adds "And they were saying many other things against Him, blaspheming" (22:65).

Moreover, the guards took Him and beat Him. By dawn, His face and body would be black and blue. Jesus probably spent the rest of the night tied in an uncomfortable posture to the pillars and walls in the dungeon below the palace.[14]

The Trial Before the Sanhedrin

The priests attempted a hurried, postdawn trial with the larger assembly of the Sanhedrin to give the sentence some semblance of legality. Twenty-three members constituted a quorum, and since "the whole Sanhedrin" (a quorum) agreed on the verdict, Joseph of Arimathea and Nicodemus were probably not present. This was probably the smaller Sanhedrin of twenty-three members.[15] Technically, a capital trial could only commence after the morning sacrifice, held between daybreak and sunrise.[16] Earlier authorities thought this trial was conducted in the Hall of Hewn Stones, the usual meeting place of the Sanhedrin,[17] but we cannot be certain.

This trial was a sham. No witnesses were called. They wasted no time getting to the essential issue. They enjoined Jesus, "If You are the Christ, tell us" (Luke 22:67). Now with the entire court present to hear, Jesus answered them, "If I tell you, you will not believe; and if I ask a question, you will not answer. But from now on, the Son of Man will be seated at the right hand of the power of God" (vv. 67–69). He had clearly applied the Messianic passage, Psalm 110:1, to Himself.

To authenticate the verdict they were seeking, the priests asked, "Are You the Son of God, then?" Jesus answered, "Yes, I am" (Luke 22:70). Jesus had clearly, by their standard, incriminated Himself. Jewish legal practice of the day probably required that the Sanhedrin wait one full day before pronouncing a capital sentence. During that day the jurists were to fast and mourn before condemning a man to death.[18] However, the real decision had been reached during the night at the illegal trial in Caiaphas's house. The priests announced that no further witnesses were necessary.

The Civil Trials

The First Trial Before Pilate

Within the Roman Empire capital punishment was exclusively a Roman prerogative,[19] although at times the Israelites took the law into their own hands. However, collusion between the higher level of priests and the Romans had sunk to such nefarious depths that the priests apparently expected no problem from the Roman governor, Pontius Pilate. They marched Jesus, still bound, to the Lithostratom, Pilate's courtyard of huge flagstones beneath the Fortress Antonia, the Roman military head-quarters.[20] By this time exhaustion and dehydration had begun their deadly work of severely weakening Christ's body.[21]

The priests obviously expected Pilate simply to endorse their sentence. But Pilate shocked them. He demanded, "What accusation do you bring against this Man?" (John 18:29). The priests, again caught unprepared, responded weakly, "If this Man were not an evildoer, we would not have delivered Him up to you" (v. 30).

The sarcasm of Pilate's reply indicates his attitude toward their presumption: "Take Him yourselves, and judge Him according to your law" (v. 31). The evil intentions of the priests became evident as they protested that they could not execute capital punishment. Their murderous intentions required that the Roman government prosecute.

Now they had to present charges that would require civil punishment. Again they were unprepared. Their own conviction had been based on religious charges. Initially they gave the flimsy charge that Jesus misled the nation. If this were a charge of heresy, it meant nothing to a Roman, so they realized the necessity of a new, civil charge. They told Pilate that Jesus had forbade the payment of taxes to Caesar (Luke 23:2). This snatching at such a feeble straw must have amused Pilate. He may have known it to be a lie (Luke 20:25). They finally pounced on a substantial allegation, they told Pilate that Jesus had claimed to be "Christ, a King" (Luke 23:2).

Such a charge was quite serious in the Roman Empire. Pilate, knowing that the priests would not enter a Gentile residence for fear of defilement on a high feast day, went into the Praetorium to question Jesus privately. As a prisoner, Jesus was inside the fortress. Pilate summoned Jesus and asked Him, "Are you the King of the Jews?" (John 18:33).

Jesus challenged Pilate to think: "Are you saying this on your own initiative, or did others tell you about Me?" (v. 34). Pilate refused the challenge. He replied, "I am not a Jew, am I? Your own nation and the chief priests delivered You up to me; what have You done?" (v. 35). Jesus answered, "My kingdom is not of this world. If My kingdom were of this world, then My servants would be fighting, that I might not be delivered up to the Jews; but as it is, My kingdom is not of this realm" (v. 36).

Pilate, uncomprehending, was nonplused. He could only exclaim, "So You are a king?" Jesus further elucidated the spiritual nature of His kingship as far as Pilate could understand: "You say correctly that I am a king. For this I have been born, and for this I have come into the world, to bear witness to the truth. Every one who is of the truth hears My voice" (v. 37). The Gentile Pilate could not comprehend the profoundly spiritual nature of Jesus' claim, but he discerned by now that Jesus had no political pretensions. Taking Jesus with him, he went to the priests and announced, "I find no guilt in Him" (v. 38).

This unexpected verdict addled the frustrated priests. Stymied again, they accused Jesus of many things. Pilate was caught between the power of the priests and the obvious innocence of Jesus. He asked Jesus, "Do You make no answer? See how many charges they bring against You!" (Mark 15:4). Matthew tells us that the dignified refusal of Jesus to respond to this intense hatred greatly amazed Pilate (27:14).

In their frenzied accusations, the priests inadvertently opened a way of escape for the trapped governor. They added to their allegations, "He stirs up the people, teaching all over Judea, starting from Galilee, even as far as this place" (Luke 23:5). Pilate's nervous alertness caught the mention of a Galilean origin. He demanded to know if Jesus were, in fact, a Galilean. They assured him that Jesus was.

The relieved Pilate immediately grasped at this faint hope. He saw a chance to kill two birds with one stone. He and Herod Antipas, the tetrarch of Galilee, had been at odds with each other. Antipas had sent the emperor a letter of protest over Pilate's importation of some shields bearing an image of the emperor.[22] Pilate knew that Antipas was in Jerusalem for the Passover. Here was a gesture he could make to Herod that would, at the same time, get this case off his hands. He sent Jesus to the man who may well be the cheapest character in the New Testament.

The Trial Before Herod

Herod Antipas was a contemptible man with a bizarre imagination. He had kept Jesus' cousin, John the Baptist, in prison for months. He was afraid of John, but at the same time fascinated with him. He was also puzzled by John's message, "but he used to enjoy listening to him" (Mark 6:20). Then Herod's wife (who had married him illicitly) tricked him into injudiciously ordering the execution of the prophet. He had even imagined that Jesus' extraordinary powers were the result of a resurrection of John the Baptist (Mark 6:16).

In his fear, Herod had tried to threaten Jesus, who refused to be intimidated (Luke 13:31–32). The mystical and the unusual fascinated Herod, for he had wanted to see Jesus for a long time. He hoped to see one of the supernatural works of this miracle worker. He was, in other words, a vulgar and coarse person.

The angry priests pursued their prey into Herod's court. They continued their accusations vehemently. In his brutish curiosity, Herod himself plied Jesus with many questions. Jesus' elegant nobility surely recoiled from the vileness of this ignoble scene. He was faced with the killer of His cousin and with the continued false charges of the blood-thirsty priests. Herod Antipas is the only character Jesus ever met to whom He spoke not one word. He did not give Herod the satisfaction of answers to charges He need not deny and vacuous questions offensive to His dignity.

Herod could have pursued the matter, but he demonstrated no confidence in the face of the composure of Jesus. He had, after all, been tricked into beheading the prophet and had suffered the popular hatred of the people because of it. He did not need the execution of another prophet on his record. Furthermore, his old enemy, Pilate, had deferred to him. Rather than embroil himself in a situation he might not handle well, Herod decided to defer to Pilate. In what must have been frustration and disappointment, he turned Jesus over to his own soldiers, who mockingly dressed Him elegantly (possibly in the white robe of Jewish royalty) and made sport of His stately behavior. But Jesus was on His way back to the Roman governor of Judea.

The Second Trial Before Pilate

Pilate now found himself in a quandary. Jesus was obviously innocent. Even Herod had not been able to substantiate a charge. Yet the vociferous priests would not relent in their pursuit of a Roman execution. Pilate's wife sent a message to him that she had "suffered greatly in a dream because of Him" (Matt. 27:19). Almost certainly God had caused this dream, but she perhaps thought that one of the many Roman gods had spoken to her. If, however, she knew something of Jesus, as her dream suggests, Pilate also probably had some basic information on the prisoner.

Pilate saw some chance of a surrogate choice in the annual custom of releasing a prisoner at Passover. However, the early morning crowd was probably made up of Judeans, not Galileans. The Judeans had never followed Christ, and it was not difficult for the priests to persuade the rabble to ask for Barabbas rather than Jesus.

Still determined to release Jesus, Pilate made yet another appeal to the priests, but they again demanded Jesus' death. Pilate told them, "Why, what evil has this man done? I have found in Him no guilt demanding death; I will therefore punish Him and release Him" (Luke 23:22).

This was no idle threat. Although flogging normally preceded crucifixion,[23] in this case Pilate was hoping that such an appalling punishment would satisfy the angry priests and that crucifixion itself could be avoided.[24]

The Scourging

So many died from this punishment that it was called the "half-death."[25] From one to six lictors (Roman officers) administered the punishment, and they alternated positions during the flogging.[26] The victim was tied to a stake. The usual instrument was a flagrum to which were attached several braided leather thongs. Horace calls it the "horrible flagellum."[27] Knots were tied into the ends of each thong, and sheep bone or balls of lead were inserted into the knots.

Jewish whipping was limited to thirty-nine stripes. According to Deuteronomy 25:3, the legal limit was forty lashes, but the fortieth stripe was left out in case of a miscount (see 2 Cor. 11:24). Roman scourging had no set limit; its limit was the skill of the lictor, who was medically trained. The object was to bring the victim as close to death as possible. Many victims died from this punishment,[28] and when they died no blame was attached to the lictors. They were, after all, administering the half-death.

The object of the balls in the thongs was to bruise, and with deft twists of the thongs the lictors could cut open the bruises they were making. The continued lacerations tore into the underlying skeletal muscles and so ripped and cleaved the skin of the back that it hung in quivering ribbons of bleeding flesh.[29] Blood loss would be intense, initially from the capillaries and veins, but finally from the arteries themselves as the muscles were torn open.[30] At times, even the entrails were laid bare.[31]

The victim normally fainted after about two and a half minutes. The lictor would walk over, count the pulse and check the respiration. If he could feel a pulse, he would continue the scourging.[32] Nevertheless, the intense pain and excessive blood loss had set the stage for circulatory shock. The amount of blood loss contributed to the length of time the victim survived on the cross.[33] The wording of 1 Peter 2:24 indicates that the scourging of Jesus was particularly harsh.[34] Hematidrosis and its attendant adverse effects had rendered Jesus especially vulnerable to the scourging's negative effects on His circulatory system.[35] This partially explains the short duration of Jesus' time on the cross; His blood supply was already greatly spent.

The Roman soldiers now realized that they had an amazing example of toughness on their hands. Small wonder He claimed to be a king. And yet, hardy as He was, He was in the hands of mighty Rome. The soldiers wanted to have some real sport of this extraordinary man, this rural Jew, come to the religious capital and claiming to be a king, so they decided to have a "coronation."

The Roman royal color was purple. One of the soldiers found a purple robe, possibly a castoff, and draped it around the bleeding shoulders and back of Jesus. The blood would have clotted quickly, and the matted robe would have clung tightly to the lacerated body.

The Romans crowned their Caesar with laurel, but these soldiers did not use laurel. The men plaited a crown of thorns, probably from the kindling used in the fireplace of the fortress. The head is a very vascular area, and the extreme blood loss was rendered more acute as the soldiers "crowned" Jesus. They repeatedly struck Him in the face and on the head with a staff as they jeered, "Hail, King of the Jews!" (John 19:3). To add insult to injury, they spit on Him.

This was the pitiable specimen Pilate presented back to the priests, thinking that now, surely, they would have mercy. He informed them, "Behold, I am bringing Him out to you, that you may know that I find no guilt in Him" (John 19:4). As Jesus came out, Pilate cried, "Behold, the Man!" (v. 5, *idou ho anthropos*). The priests, maddened from their long wait, were driven to screaming. They shouted, "Crucify! Crucify!" (v. 6). Pilate once again attempted to turn the case back over to them as a religious case: "Take Him yourselves, and crucify Him, for I find no guilt in Him" (v. 6).

Once again stymied, the priests, frustrated by the six long trials, finally conceded their real motive. At long last the truth was inexorably exposed: "We have a law, and by that law He ought to die because He made Himself out to be the Son of God" (v. 7).

This revelation completely changed the complexion of Pilate's attitude. His wife had warned him of her dream. John tells us that at this point he was "the more afraid" (19:8). To get Jesus away from the priests, he took Jesus into the safety of the fortress once again and demanded, "Where are You from?" (v. 9).

Jesus had told a Hebrew multitude of His heavenly origin (John 6:38), and they had had many hundreds of years of prophecy to prepare them for the Messiah's coming. Yet with all their knowledge of Scripture, they had not understood. Jesus knew that this Gentile with no background in Scripture could not possibly understand, and so He simply waited in stately silence for Pilate to proceed. Pilate, exasperated, demanded, "You do not speak to me? Do You not know that I have authority to release You, and I have authority to crucify You?" (John 19:10).

Jesus did answer this. With unbelievable presence of mind, He assured Pilate, "You would have no authority over Me, unless it had been given you from above; for this reason he who delivered Me up to you has the greater sin" (v. 11). This serene answer convinced Pilate that he must somehow free Jesus. He led Jesus out and began once again to try to reason with the priests. The priests, exhausted by the long hours of fruitless haggling, now knew that they were forced to use their ultimate strategy —blackmail.

They knew that Pilate's job as governor had been secured for him by the prefect of the Roman Praetorian Guard, a close counselor to Tiberius Caesar, and the second-most-powerful man in the empire, Lucius Aelius Sejanus.[36] Now, after an abortive attempt to seize Tiberius' throne, Pilate's protector in Rome, Sejanus, was dead, executed for high treason.[37] Without his protector, Pilate was in jeopardy with Tiberius.

Rome had two kinds of provinces, those at the disposal of the senate, or senatorial provinces, and those directly under the emperor, imperial provinces. Judea was an imperial province.[38] As the governor of an imperial province, Pilate was considered one of the *amici Caesaris,* or "friends of Caesar."[39] This enviable position had now been threatened by the dishonorable death of Sejanus.

Pilate had had difficulties with the Jewish religion from the beginning. He probably had been influenced by the anti-Semitic prejudices of Sejanus.[40] Pilate had earlier brought some standards emblazoned with images of Caesar into Jerusalem. These "graven images" were an affront to the Jews, who rushed to his residence in Caesarea and begged him to remove the standards. When he refused, crowds remained prone around his house for five days and nights. Pilate summoned the mob to the great stadium in Caesarea and threatened to cut them to pieces. The Jews flung themselves to the ground and bent their necks to receive the blows. Pilate acquiesced and ordered the standards removed.[41]

Later he wanted to build an aqueduct and dipped into the Jewish temple treasury to finance his project. Again mobs of people crowded around his tribunal. Pilate ordered some of his soldiers to infiltrate the crowd with civilian clothing over their armor. At a signal, the soldiers began beating the rioters. Large numbers died or were trampled to death in the ensuing flight.[42] Pilate's entire record with the Jews had been poor from the beginning.

The priests knew that Pilate's position in the Roman empire was threatened in two important ways—his friendship with the traitorous

Sejanus and his inglorious performance in Judea. They taunted him, "If you release this Man, you are no friend of Caesar [the Latin form, *amicus Caesaris*, referred to his position as governor]; every one who makes himself out to be a king opposes Caesar" (John 19:12).

An uproar was breaking out, and Pilate had managed such chaos very poorly in the past. He knew he was defeated. He washed his hands in front of the crowd to demonstrate his determined insistence on Jesus' innocence, walked to the judgment seat, the *sella curulis*[43] (in Greek, the *bema*), to pronounce the official sentence, *Pone crucem servo* ("Put the cross on the slave").[44] The governor could not say "Put the slave on the cross" because the victim was required to carry the crossbeam, the *patibulum*, along a winding procession through the streets of Jerusalem. Each victim had to carry his own cross. Pilate then remembered that two other criminals were awaiting execution and ordered their deaths.

Roman Execution

Now began the dread preparations for the long walk to the execution site, the Place of the Skull—Golgotha (Greek version of the Aramaic *Gulgata*) or Calvary (Latin version of the Greek *kranion*, a skull). The soldiers ripped the clotted robe from the torn back and shoulders of Jesus.

Jesus had been weakened by the long walks to the various trials; lack of food, water, and sleep; severe loss of blood; and the excruciating flogging. His physical condition now was at least serious and possibly critical.[45] The victim's arms were stretched the length of the patibulum, and this crossbar was lashed with cords to the shoulders, the arms, and the hands.[46] The patibulum weighed between 75 and 125 pounds.[47]

At last began the rigorous walk to the Place of the Skull. As an example to anyone who would dare to cross Rome, the victims were forced to carry the patibulum through a narrow and twisting procession that has come to be known as the *Via Dolorosa* ("Way of Sorrows").

Roman crucifixion was more cruel than other forms, and the victims tried to hold back. The soldiers had to force the victims forward. To do this, they tied a rope around his waist. By pulling on the rope when the victim held back, they could jerk the prisoner onward.[48] Because of the preceding protracted tortures and the extreme weakening of His forces, Jesus was undoubtedly moving very slowly and probably staggering under the enormous weight.

Tradition tells us that under the determined urging of the soldiers, He fell. This is almost certainly true, for the soldiers had to force a pilgrim from the wayside, Simon of Cyrene, to carry the cross the rest of the way—an unusual procedure in the crucifixion process. The fall drove the thorns deeper into His brow, since Jesus' arms were lashed to the patibulum and He could not brace for the fall.

The Crucifixion

The Jews hated crucifixion. They executed criminals principally by stoning and several other methods. A society of Jewish women had secured permission to give crucifixion victims a drug to deaden the pain.[49] They did this when the procession arrived at the Place of the Skull. The two thieves accepted their potion, but Jesus refused His. He wanted His mind clear and His faculties focused. He knew what He was doing.

They flung Him into the dirt, pebbles, and grime of the hillside and stretched His arms onto the patibulum. The spikes were driven, not through the palm, but through the wrist, at the heel of the hand. Ancient peoples considered the wrist to be a part of the hand.[50] A nail through the palm cannot support the weight of the body; also, by driving the nail at a precise point through the wrist, they could aggravate the median nerve.

From that point on, a never-ending trail of fire raced up and down the victim's arms; the only relief the victim could know from this agony was death.[51] The spikes they used were square in shape, about 5.5 inches long and about a third of an inch across at the top.[52] This nailing causes the thumb to be drawn sharply inward; it strikes the palm, and as the process continues, the fingers also are cramped sharply inward.[53]

Several upright bars were kept planted in place at the Place of the Skull. This beam, the *stipes,* was sharpened at the top, like a pencil. In each patibulum, a hollowed-out cup was carved. Using ropes and ladders, the soldiers could lift the nailed victim and implant the hollowed-out cup onto the sharpened end of the stipes, like a mortise and tenon.[54] The lifting of the body would finally sever the median nerve, creating a lightning shot of pain in the arms. Christ was placed on the center cross probably because His was the chief "crime."[55] The *titulus* ("placard") describing His "crime" read, "Jesus the Nazarene, the King of the Jews" (John 19:19).

Nails were not necessary to cause death. The Egyptians, in fact, used ropes to fasten the victim to the cross,[56] but Rome was more cruel and preferred nails. The arms were nailed at ninety degrees, but in the course of hanging on the cross, the body would sag to sixty-five degrees. The weight of the body fixed certain breathing muscles in an inhalation state and hindered passive exhalation.[57] In other words, the pectoral muscles became paralyzed and the victim discovered that he could breathe in, but not out. The usual cause of death in crucifixion was asphyxiation and shock from loss of blood.[58]

If they did not nail the feet, the victim died quickly. Prior to death the victim flailed his body and irritated the guards. The Romans had discovered a way to prevent this flailing and to prolong the agony. They bent the knees to a twenty-degree angle, slammed one foot against the stipes, folded the other foot over it, and drove an additional spike through the second metatarsal space of the feet.

The Romans were such experts that they could predict within four hours how long a man would live on the cross by the angle they used in bending the knees.[59] This nail injured the peroneal nerve and branches of the medial and lateral plantar nerves; the periosteum, the membrane of highly innervated connective tissue with numerous blood vessels surrounding the bones of the feet, would be stripped off, creating intense pain.[60]

As the victim hung there, unable to breathe, tetany, a condition marked by cramps and contractions of the muscles, would set in.[61] A profound lack of oxygen and the inability to exhale carbon dioxide caused the tetany. The victim would discover that, if he used the nail going through his feet as a cruel step to force his body upward so that the arms once more reached a ninety-degree angle, he could breathe again. Each time Christ spoke, He had to do this.

He alternately hung by the nails in His hands until the need for oxygen forced Him to stand on the spike in His feet.[62] This inevitably reopened the wounds in His feet, causing further loss of blood and also greatly exacerbated the wounds in His back as He slid up and down on the rough wood of the stipes.

"There they crucified Him" (Luke 23:33). By Jewish reckoning, the crucifixion took place at the "third hour" (Mark 15:25), or about nine o'clock in the morning. To the Jews, death by crucifixion, or the hanging of a body on a tree, was particularly odious. It indicated a curse (Deut. 21:23). To the Romans also, death by crucifixion was shameful, and they later considered the worship of one crucified a monstrosity.[63]

Crucifixion was a horrific, disgusting business and is seldom mentioned in Roman inscriptions and writings.[64] Paul accurately described the attitude of the ancient world when he said that the cross was "to Jews a stumbling block, and to Gentiles foolishness" (1 Cor. 1:23). Jesus took upon Himself not only the divine shame of sin but the human humiliation and disgrace associated with this hateful form of death.

Early in the process, Jesus forced His weight up on the foot spike and prayed, "Father, forgive them; for they do not know what they are doing" (Luke 23:34). His first word from the cross was not for Himself.

The mob began to insult Him and to shake their heads, saying, "You who are going to destroy the temple and rebuild it in three days, save Yourself! If You are the Son of God, come down from the cross" (Matt. 27:40). Obviously this information from the trial had been passed out by the priests or other members of the Sanhedrin. The priests themselves mocked Him, saying, "He saved others; He cannot save Himself. Let this Christ, the King of Israel, now come down from the cross, so that we may see and believe!" (Mark 15:31–32).

Of course He could have come down. He could have called legions of angels to deliver Him from this dishonor and from the anguish of crucifixion. But He did not do that. With such unmatchable power available to Him that He could create this enormous universe, He did not come down. What motive could hold Him, the power of the universe, bound to this shame and mortification? For God so loved . . .

As He hung there, His muscles stood out in rigid, involuntary cramps.[65] The difficulty of the blood flow through the body caused headaches and possibly convulsions.[66] His body became soaked with perspiration. From loss of blood and perspiration, dehydration was extreme and thirst became intense.[67]

Crucifixion victims also suffered the annoyance of insects drawn to the blood and smells. Jesus had to endure hours of twisting, joint-rending cramps, partial intermittent asphyxiation, and fiery sting in His back as He moved up and down against the timber of the stipes.[68] Pain and shock were extreme.

Jesus' second word from the cross also was not for Himself. The Holy Spirit did a remarkable work in one of the thieves, who asked to be remembered in Jesus' kingdom. Jesus told him, "Truly I say to you, today you shall be with Me in Paradise" (Luke 23:43). His third word was also not of Himself as He committed the care of His mother to the apostle John (John 19:26–27).

The Darkness

Finally, about noon ("the sixth hour," Mark 15:33), came the dread moment for which Jesus had sweated blood. By now the whole of His holy being was dreadfully, terribly gripped by all the filth, dirt, and slime of our sins—a distress far worse than any of the outward, physical anguish. God "made Him who knew no sin to be sin on our behalf" (2 Cor. 5:21). Jesus was now ugly. He was hideously deformed, repulsive, and repugnant. He was guilty, although it was our guilt He was bearing. He was sin.

The most terrible moment in the history of the universe had arrived. God the Holy Father cannot gaze upon sin. Out of the need consistent with His perfect holiness, God had to turn away from His only begotten Son.[69] In this appalling moment, the perfect continuum of ceaseless and ageless unbroken love was suddenly split by a gigantic rip, a horrible tear in the flawless fabric of absolute love. Perfect love was painfully torn by an awesome rupture for the first and only time in all eternity. Jesus was now in the hell of exile from God.

This hell had two dread factors. The first was isolation. Not even the most isolated missionary today knows the awesome loneliness of that isolation, because the missionary is not separated from God as Jesus was from His Father. Solitary confinement is a frightful punishment. God created us to need our fellows because, in His love, His nature is to share. But even in solitary, the Christian is not alone, for God is with Him. None of us can appreciate the evil that is total aloneness, that outermost point of utter desolation.

The second factor that made this hell terrible beyond our knowing was guilt. The horror of guilt is its condemnation. Condemnation is final. No appeal can be made from condemnation. Guilt is also helpless and irreversible. Guilt is powerless to help itself. Jesus deliberately remained powerless so that we would have the power to accept His work. We are not helpless in our guilt because He was. He had to accept helplessness if we were to be redeemed. In these terrible moments, all the fury of offended absolute holiness was poured out on the vileness of our guilt, then on His shoulders.

If God the Father cannot look at Jesus, no other human being will be allowed to see the awesome sacrifice into which Jesus had entered. God drew a curtain of night across the earth, and suddenly it was dark. Tertullian says that this "wonder is related in your own annals and is preserved in your archives to this day."[70] Merchants working in the little market stalls were suddenly interrupted; they could not see to do business. The priests preparing sacrifices in the temple now groped in the darkness.

Darkness covered all the land (Matt. 27:45; Mark 15:33; Luke 23:44). The stars could be seen.[71] This darkness could not have been an eclipse, for the sun cannot be eclipsed at the full moon of the Passover.[72] The darkness was a miracle, a momentous and critically important work of God.

Now Jesus was isolated, dreadfully alone, guilty, and condemned. He had to suffer this torment in utter darkness, itself a curse (Exod. 10:21–23). No other human being had ever known what He now knew. And because He did it, no other human being need know what He knew in these hours. He became a curse for us (Gal. 3:13).

Normally the brain will not accept severe trauma; it blacks out. If the brain refuses to faint for some unknown reason, the stomach pours gastric juices and blood into the abdominal cavity. This gastric dilatation extends from the neck to the hips.[73] His body was now hideous, deformed into a repugnant, bloated mass. "His appearance was marred more than any man, And His form more than the sons of men" (Isa. 52:14).

His sacrifice was that of a perfect man; His suffering was that of an infinite God, and as such was infinite. None of us can ever know, we can only inadequately appreciate the infinity of this cosmic suffering.

The tiniest hint of what He went through is seen in His cry as God lifted the darkness after three hours (Luke 23:44)—"My God, My God, why hast Thou forsaken Me?" (Mark 15:34)—a quotation of Psalm 22:1, the great Crucifixion Psalm that details the rigors of the crucifixion about a thousand years before Christ's death. Jesus, who can only speak truth, said that God had forsaken Him.

The Climax

By this time, Jesus' heart was struggling to pump the small amount of blood left in His torn and lacerated system. In these final desperate stages, according to some medical authorities, blood serum began to engorge the pericardium, the sac of thin membrane that surrounds the heart. With this came a deep, crushing pain in the chest cavity. The squeezed heart now was laboring to pump heavy, thick, sluggish blood through the maimed and sorely abused body.[74]

By now the day was late, possibly a little after three o'clock. For legal reasons His death needed to come quickly for His body to be buried prior to sundown. Yet before He could die, He had to make an important announcement. No one could make this declaration but Jesus, and the Father was waiting to hear Him say it.

But He could not speak. Long hours ago His body was tortured by extreme dehydration. His throat and mouth were parched, and His tongue was wooden from thirst. But He had to speak. Eternity hinged on His utterance of this one word. Struggling, He managed to say: "I am thirsty" (John 19:28). One of the soldiers ran to his pack and soaked a sponge in *posca,* a cheap, sour vinegar that soldiers carried at the time.[75]

Jesus took enough to moisten His lips, mouth, and tongue, and finally, at long last, with His mouth now slightly loosened, came the mighty and consummating word God had been waiting to hear: "It is finished!" (John 19:30). And it really *is* finished.

Jesus never did anything halfway. He did not heal halfway; no leper ever approached Him after being healed and complained, "I seem to have these white spots again." His teaching was so profound that the greatest minds have spent lifetimes trying to unravel all its secrets and yet a child may understand its essentials. Jesus did not do anything halfway, and He certainly did not redeem halfway. He paid in its entirety the enormous debt for all the sin against holiness that the rest of us incurred. Jesus paid it all.

The work was over now. Astonishingly, He called out His final cry from the cross in a loud voice, indicating the strength He still had. He had been in control when the band of priests obeyed Him in Gethsemane. At the end, He is still in control. He prayed, "Father, into Thy hands I commit My spirit" (Luke 23:46). The fact that He committed His spirit indicates an act of the will. Jesus dismissed His spirit. He had said, "No one has taken it [life] away from Me, but I lay it down on My own initiative. I have authority to lay it down, and I have authority to take it up again" (John 10:18).[76]

What happened next would be described by a modern novelist as saying that "His head pitched forward." John, who normally records in his Gospel the things he saw, tells us that "He *bowed* His head" (John 19:30, emphasis added). His last act was an act of submission. He breathed His last breath and gave up (John 19:30, *paradidomi*) His spirit. The lungs stopped their functioning, and the struggling heart finally stopped. He was dead.

As the frightened followers watched the gray body slump into life-lessness, looking at the blood-stained corpse, they found it very hard to remember anything Jesus had said about resurrection. But He had said it, and His words always came true.

The Cross Changes Lives

All of God's actions, like God's attributes, are absolutes. The Old Testament sacrifices were incomplete; they could not perform the work of atonement. But Jesus' sacrifice finishes the need for blood sacrifice forever for it is an absolute. "By this will [of God] we have been sancti-fied through the offering of the body of Jesus Christ once for all. And every priest stands daily ministering and offering time after time the same sacrifices, which can never take away sins; but He, having offered one sacrifice for sins for all time, sat down at the right hand of God, waiting from that time onward until His enemies be made a footstool for His feet. *For by one offering He has perfected for all time those who are sanctified*" (Heb. 10:10–14, emphasis added).

The work of the cross was to atone for our sins. Atonement itself is life changing. Without the cross, redemption would have been beyond price. Yet redemption is free through the atoning sacrifice of the Lord Jesus. All who accept His payment for their redemption receive all the benefits of His mighty, grand work on their behalf. They become new creatures in Christ.

The work is personally for each individual who will accept it. Accepting Christ's atonement ushers in a new birth, and with it a changed life. The totality and effectiveness of the work of the cross has been seen through the centuries in lives altered and redirected by it. The change from Saul the persecutor to Paul the apostle is dramatic, but this is typical of the changes in thousands of other lives, including mine.

This is the glory of the cross. Jesus had prayed that God would glo-rify Him (John 17:1). That glory was consummated in one whole and perfect offering. From beginning to end, Jesus was in control. He directed every detail of the transcendent sacrifice He was making. No incidental detail was omitted as the overwhelming debt of all our sins was paid so thoroughly that the absolute holiness of God was satisfied. Not only is God satisfied, but I am grateful for the life I now have in Christ. The toiling labor of the cross is glorious, and it is complete.

Holiness and love had worked together to complete the mightiest work of all eternity. God's holiness was totally satisfied. No one now could ever question His love.

Christ's death redirected history, and it redirects our lives today. We are holy and loving because His death made possible our conversion. Knowing the details of His death gives us a more thorough understanding of the price divine love paid.

Conclusion

Christ's death purchases for me an absolute and a complete redemption. My mind now is to offer my own sacrifice, however incomplete and insignificant it may be. God's goal is the completion of my sanctification and the perfection of my love. My measure for holiness and love is the payment Jesus made for me. He paid my debt in His office as Redeemer. Because of Him, I will sanctify what He sanctifies and love what He loves. He changed my life.

chapter ten

Raised from the Dead

Wherefore also God hath highly exalted him

More miracles are recorded in the hours surrounding Christ's death, burial, and resurrection than any other comparable period in the Bible. The strange midday darkness certainly made a profound impression on the inhabitants of Jerusalem. At the moment of Christ's death an earthquake shook the earth and huge rocks split open. Tombs were opened and out of them came, after Christ's resurrection, saints who appeared to the local inhabitants.[1] The day saw terrifying upheaval.

Deep in the rear of the temple, the Holy of Holies was curtained off from the Holy Place by an enormous double curtain. The main veil was forty cubits (sixty feet) long and twenty cubits (thirty feet) high. This curtain was worked in seventy-two joined squares, each the thickness of a man's hand (about three inches) wide.[2]

Suddenly, as Christ died, this three-inch thick veil began to tear from the top down. This symbolically opened the way into the presence of God for all mankind in subsequent time. Previously, none but the high priest could enter this holiest of all earthly places, and that but once a year. Since about fifty priests were on duty in the various parts of the temple at this time,[3] news of this cataclysmic event would spread quickly across Jerusalem.

The priests were anxious to bury the crucifixion victims prior to sundown, because the Levitical law stated that if a body that had been hung on a tree were allowed to hang overnight, the land would be desecrated (Deut. 21:22–23). The Jewish day begins at evening (Gen. 1:5; Ps. 55:17), and so the burials were a matter of great urgency. The priests were anxious to hasten the process of death in the three victims on the crosses. The next day was the Sabbath. After that followed the Week of Unleavened Bread, and so burial would be impossible after sunset until the feast was finished.

The Romans had a method of hastening the death of crucifixion victims called *crura fracta*,[4] or, in its English form, "crurifracture." In crurifracture, one of the soldiers would take a heavy iron bar, a *crucifragium*, and smash the calf bones of the victim. The victim would then be unable to push his weight up on the spike in his feet and would asphyxiate quickly. This distasteful task was dreaded by the soldiers.

The soldiers crushed the legs of the two robbers, but when they came to Jesus they saw that He was already dead. Crurifracture was unnecessary. This was significant, for when Moses instituted the Passover, he forbade breaking the lamb's bones (Exod. 12:46). Later it became a permanent part of the Law (Num. 9:12). As the Lamb of God (John 1:29), Jesus knew that His legs must not be broken. Perhaps one factor in willing His death was avoiding the necessity of crurifracture.

Nevertheless, being professionals, the executioners knew that they could leave no doubt about the finality of the death of their victims, and so the soldier smashed a spear into the chest cavity of Jesus, "and immediately there came out blood and water" (John 19:34). Almost certainly this spear pierced the right auricle of the heart. Blood remains liquid in a corpse,[5] and the right auricle is always filled with blood.[6]

The hole made by the spear in the thorax was quite large, because later Thomas could have inserted his hand into it (John 20:27). The water that John mentioned was the serum that had accumulated in the pericardium and perhaps the gastric juices from the gastric dilatation.[7] The heart itself, therefore, was cut open. John, an eyewitness, recorded this detail so that no medical doubt could remain that Jesus was actually dead.

Annas had asked about high-ranking members of the Sanhedrin who were disciples. Jesus did actually have some high-ranking disciples. One of these, Joseph of Arimathea, was "a prominent member of the Council" (Mark 15:43). Arimathea was a village about twenty miles northwest of Jerusalem.[8] Joseph probably had served first in the local synagogue of Arimathea, and then, because of his piety and possibly his wealth, he had been promoted to serve on the national Sanhedrin. The disciples could not have secured an audience with Pilate. However, because of his rank, Joseph was able to request permission to bury Jesus.

Normally the Romans left crucified corpses to the carrion birds, but because of the great sensitivities of the Jews to such matters, Caesar Augustus had granted them permission to bury the victims who were certified as dead.[9] Pilate granted Joseph permission. In this way, God prevented a criminal burial, for often the bodies of criminals were consigned to be burned in the Valley of Gehenna.[10] Joseph was joined by Nicodemus, also a member of the Sanhedrin (John 3:1), who had first come to the Lord secretly and had remained a secret disciple. To Joseph and Nicodemus fell the unpleasant task of disengaging the corpse from the stipes and the patibulum.

In doing this, they demonstrated willingness to take on Levitical defilement; Numbers 19:11 decreed that "the one who touches the corpse of any person shall be unclean for seven days." This meant that Joseph and Nicodemus were unable to participate in any of the Feast of Unleavened Bread for the week following Passover. This public act also incriminated both Joseph and Nicodemus, separated them from the social strata they were accustomed to, and identified them irrevocably with the disciples of Jesus.

In the Gospels we can count about twenty-three persons who were in the Lord's party at the end. Luke tells us that "all His acquaintances and the women who accompanied Him from Galilee, were standing at a distance, seeing these things" (23:49). After His death, the people all departed, except for two women, Mary Magdalene and Mary the mother of James and Joses. These two women followed Joseph and Nicodemus to see the final disposition of the body. Socially, they could not mix with Joseph and Nicodemus, and custom required them to keep their distance.[11]

The procedure was first to wash the body with warm water and then rub it down with perfumed essences.[12] Because of the lateness of the hour and the rush to get the body buried prior to sundown, the evidence indicates that the men had to forego this procedure; they could not have secured the warm water quickly, and the washing is not mentioned in the Gospels.

The Egyptians embalmed; the Jews did not. The Jewish custom was to wrap the body with linen cloths impregnated with the spices of myrrh and aloes, to counteract the odor of putrefaction.[13] The Bible even tells us how they divided the expenses: Joseph paid for the linens (Mark 15:46) and Nicodemus paid for the spices, about seventy-five pounds (John 19:39). Jesus was given an expensive burial.

Although most common people buried underground at the time, the wealthy carved out tombs in the hillside and prepared a slab for the reception of the body. Joseph's own tomb happened to be near the Place of the Skull, approached by a small garden. The tomb had two chambers, first an anteroom, or vestibule, that led into the second room, the tomb proper, which contained the slab for the body.[14] A trench was dug in front of the tomb, and then a large cylindrical stone,[15] the "Golet,"[16] was placed in the trench. They rolled the stone up the hill and placed a wedge under it to keep it in place until they had a body for burial. Joseph's tomb had never been used.

The two Marys watched as Jesus' body was deposited on the slab in the tomb. Finally the burial was complete, and the stone was rolled over the entrance. A smaller stone, the "Dopheq," probably was wedged against the large one for additional security.[17]

Joseph, Nicodemus, and the two Marys would have departed to their own residing places, but certainly not to sleep. This singular night in Jerusalem was certainly not a night for sleep. The unusual circumstances of the day—the peculiar midday darkness, the earthquake, the downward tearing of the temple veil, and above all, the ghastly death of the much-loved prophet, Jesus of Nazareth—all contributed to the strangeness of this incredible night. Tranquilizers were not known at that time, and the disciples, the friends of Jesus, and the general populace were surely greatly agitated.

The Sabbath

Any Sabbath in Judea was a high, holy day. The Passover Sabbath was one of the highest and holiest days of the year. John calls it a "high day" (19:31; the Greek states, "great was the day of that Sabbath"). With the profound shock and grief from the death of Jesus, we can be quite sure that as dawn came to the city, a pall and a gloom hung over the buildings.

The disciples observed the Sabbath; the priests did not. The priests went to Pilate and informed him of Jesus' claim that He would rise again after three days. These enemies of Jesus remembered something that the disciples had forgotten. Somehow, although He had predicted these events all along, His disciples had not been able to take in their reality and meaning. They had been blinded by their hopes for an immediate earthly kingdom. Because of their encounters with Jesus' incredible power, their attention had been fixed on a worldly glory, so much so that Jesus' words did not sink in. Their enemies were more cunning (wickedness always is). The priests and the Pharisees wanted to safeguard what they believed to be their accomplishment.

The priests asked Pilate for a guard to keep the disciples from stealing the body and then claiming that Jesus had been resurrected from the dead. Pilate told them that they had a guard and ordered the securing of the tomb. They placed a seal, probably of clay or wax, on the two stones so that any disturbance would be immediately apparent—and Jesus Christ became the first person in history to be guarded to keep Him in His grave.

This Sabbath was the most difficult day in the life of the eleven disciples and the small group of women. First of all, they were grieving profoundly. Never had they known a love like Jesus had shown them (John 13:1, 15:9). Jesus' winsomeness was entirely a spiritual attractiveness, and these men and women were sensitive spiritually. Jesus had recognized and acknowledged their love (John 14:15, 23, 28), yet He was dead. On this dark Sabbath, they buried themselves in their sorrow.

Second, they were extremely disappointed. From the beginning, in spite of Jesus' repeated emphases on the spiritual nature of His kingdom, they had envisaged what every Jew of the time had imagined —a conquering Messiah to expel Rome from Palestine and set up a splendid, visible political kingdom like that of Solomon. Even as late as the night of the betrayal, they were quarreling over their relative greatness in that new government. These high hopes were now dashed. The hated Romans had succeeded in putting to death the man they thought was invincible. They had actually attributed omniscience to Him the night before He died (John 16:30).

The Sabbath ended officially with the appearance of the third star in the sky.[18] Once the sun had set, the Jews used the remaining time of fading daylight for business. The shops opened for about an hour and a half or for two hours. The women used this time to prepare for the washing that Joseph and Nicodemus had been unable to do. They could also anoint the body with their own spices. Mary Magdalene, Mary the mother of James and Joses, and Salome went to the shops and purchased the spices in preparation for the legitimate work of the following morning. The women, possibly about nine of them, agreed to meet at the tomb the next morning,[19] not knowing what God had in store for them on this night of all nights.

The Discovery of the Resurrection

The one event in this story that I would enjoy most describing to you is the actual event of the resurrection, but I cannot. In God's wisdom, He has chosen to shroud that part of the story in the secrecy of His own wisdom. Nothing is recorded of the specific event of the resurrection. All we know is that the only man who was guarded to keep him in his grave is the only man who came out of his grave on his own volition. The most tremendous burst of divinely directed energy the world has ever known restored life and created a new body, still related to His old body, for the Lord Jesus.

The priests had taunted Him, "Let Him now come down from the cross, and we shall believe in Him" (Matt. 27:42). Jesus could have done that, but He did not. He determined to consummate the glory of His own sacrifice. He planned to do something even more spectacular and awesome than descending from the cross. He planned to come out of the grave—and He did that. Yet no one knew it.

But God knew it. If the event of the resurrection is to be cloaked in the mystery of God's secret counsels, the fact of the resurrection is not. God now shook the ground around the tomb; Matthew says the earth-quake was "violent," enough to startle and frighten the guards. Then to demonstrate the emptiness of the tomb, God sent an angel with an important mission. The dark of the morning was suddenly brightened by uncanny light. "And his appearance was like lightning, and his garment as white as snow" (Matt. 28:3). The earthquake and the glowing creature were too much for the guards, who "became like dead men" (Matt. 28:4), that is, they fainted dead away, a natural reaction to such tumultuous events.

The angel rolled the stone back, probably even out of the trench. The angel's next act had great significance: he took his seat on the stone, guarding it and defying all the powers of hell to put that stone back over the entrance. The guards awakened, surely hoping they had had a nightmare.

As they regained consciousness and looked around, the radiant creature was still there, guarding the stone. The tomb was now unmis-takably empty, and these terrified soldiers were dealing, not with fright-ened disciples, but with a creature who was manifestly supernatural. They had been paid to guard the grave, but Matthew reports that they decided not to fight. They rushed into the city, and suddenly the pall and gloom was disturbed by the footsteps of hysterical men on the cobblestones.

The men reported to the chief priests, who called a hurried meeting of the Sanhedrin. The elders did not question the absence of the body nor did they investigate the empty tomb. They recognized that they were out of control. Significantly, in the later trials of the apostles in the Book of Acts, they never accused the disciples of stealing the body. We can only imagine the dark thoughts in their minds as they grappled with a formidable reality. They bribed the soldiers to invent an absurd story of the disciples stealing the body while they were asleep. (They could not have known who stole the body if they were asleep.)

The women did not go out to the tomb together. John tells us that Mary Magdalene arrived "while it was still dark" (John 20:1). The other women, however, arrived "when the sun had risen" (Mark 16:2).[20] Mary was accompanied by "the other Mary" (mother of James and Joses; Matt. 28:1). Before their arrival, the angel moved to the interior of the tomb to await them. When Mary stepped into the garden, she saw the stone moved aside and the gaping shadowy entrance to the now-open tomb. She had expected a closed tomb, like the one she had left on the afternoon of the burial.

Immediately she thought of the expensive linen and spices, and she thought the worst—grave robbery! Fear brings out the worst in us, both in our behavior and in our psychological makeup. It had brought out the worst in the priests, and also in the disciples. In her hysteria, leaving "the other Mary" behind (a necessary conclusion from the text) to meet the larger party of women, she went running back into the city to alert Peter and John of this horrifying development.

Before the other women arrived, God sent a second angel and also stationed him inside the tomb with the first angel to meet the women. When the women were finally all together, they certainly would have known considerable unease in view of the open tomb.

When they entered the tomb and saw the angels, they were terrified. Not knowing how to react, they "bowed their faces to the ground" (Luke 24:5). One of the angels tried to calm them and verbalized their thoughts: "You are looking for Jesus the Nazarene, who has been crucified" (Mark 16:6). He then made the grand announcement, "He has risen; He is not here; behold, here is the place where they laid Him. But go, tell His disciples *and Peter,* 'He is going before you into Galilee'" (Mark 16:6–7, emphasis added). This angel gave the women special instructions to reassure Simon Peter after his tragic fall.

The second angel asked one of the most powerful questions in all of Scripture: "Why do you seek the living One among the dead?" (Luke 24:5).

He then reminded them of Jesus' own prophecy that He would die and be resurrected.

Both Mark and Matthew describe the women's run back into Jerusalem. Mark says that "trembling and astonishment had gripped them" (16:8). Matthew's words perhaps catches the spirit that they must have felt; he says they ran "with fear and great joy" (28:8). But when they told the disciples, "these words appeared to them as nonsense" (Luke 24:11). No doubt the disciples were irritable from lack of sleep and exhaustion, and they were manifesting a morbid and gloomy disbelief.

Meantime, Mary was still running. She had to go to separate houses to apprise both Peter and John of what was still to her evidence of an intolerable development to add to all the other horrors of these days. The Greek implies that she ran to Peter and to John separately (John 20:2); Jesus had predicted that they would be "scattered, each to his own home" (John 16:32). As soon as they heard the appalling news, each ran to the tomb, with Mary trailing behind. John was the younger, therefore he ran faster. But before he reached the tomb, God did a very significant thing: He removed the angels from the tomb. In His wisdom, God did not intend for the men, who were doubting, to see the angels.

John says that he did not enter the tomb but *saw* (John 20:5, *blepei*) the graveclothes. This word implies that he saw physically without understanding. When Simon Peter arrived, he went inside, and "beheld" (v. 6, *theorei*) the linens lying empty, as though the body had been simply lifted out of them. The headpiece was neatly folded apart, obviously a deliberate act. This second word for "beheld" implies that he could not make sense out of what he saw. But when John entered, he "saw [*eiden*] and believed" (v. 8); this word implies that he comprehended the significance of the empty clothes.[21] John the beloved apostle became the first human being to believe in the resurrection. The disciples left the scene with Peter in consternation and John wondering at the strange significance of these events.

The Resurrection Appearances

The First Appearance

"But Mary was standing outside the tomb weeping" (John 20:11). She may have reached the scene before the departure of Simon and John or shortly thereafter. Before she looked into the tomb, God replaced the two angels and stationed them at each end of the slab. As Mary looked in, the angels asked her, "Woman, why are you weeping?" Mary's answer indicates that her primary concern was a burial place for her Master: "Because they have taken away my Lord, and I do not know where they have laid Him" (v. 13).

As soon as she said this, she became aware of a presence in the garden with her. She turned and saw a man standing there. Her eyes were filled with tears and so she could not see clearly. By this time of day it would likely be the gardener. This man also asked the reason for her tears, but he asked something more—and note that he knows what to ask. "Whom are you seeking?" (v. 15). Mary's answer indicates the depth of her concern: "Sir, if you have carried Him away, tell me where you have laid Him, and I will take [*aro*] Him away" (v. 15). The word she used implies that she would "take up and carry away" the body herself,[22] that is, she would provide a proper burial. This also throws light onto her hysteria at the earlier discovery of the open tomb.

Having appealed to the "gardener," Mary once more turned to look at that strange configuration of empty graveclothes. But when she did that, the stranger behind her suddenly called her by name. He said it in Aramaic, the everyday language she had always spoken with Jesus: "Mary!" (v. 16). Although her eyes were filled with tears, her ears were not stuffed with cotton. Hardly able to comprehend the familiar accents she thought she had heard, Mary whirled around, and suddenly realized that she was actually seeing the solid reality of Jesus Himself, very much alive.

Her last memories had been of a bloody corpse, but this was no corpse. Jesus was alive! He Himself was standing before her. He had come to her and had called her by name. She flung herself at His feet and screamed, "Teacher!" (v. 16). The term she used, again in Aramaic, *Rabboni,* is the highest form of respect that can be paid to a teacher.[23]

Jesus reassured her, "Stop clinging to Me, for I have not yet ascended to the Father." Then He gave an important command: "Go to My brethren." The Lord then directed Mary to tell them, "I ascend to My Father." Many times she had heard Him say "My Father," but now, to her amazement, He adds, "and *your* Father, and My God and your God" (v. 17, emphasis added). The language of humanity can now demonstrate a new relationship with Jesus and with God.

One of the most amazing characteristics of the men and women who followed Jesus is their quick obedience to His orders. Whatever He commanded—"Leave your nets," "Leave your tax collecting," "Follow me," "Cross the lake," "Bring me the five loaves and the two fish"—they obeyed instantly and without question. Mary preferred to linger, but like the disciples she knew she must obey immediately. Jesus told Mary, "Go," and she went. He said, "Tell," and she told. The evidence indicates that they did not believe Mary either.

The fact that Jesus chose to appear to Mary Magdalene first is striking. By Jewish law, women were not allowed to testify in court,[24] and this may be one reason why the men found their story incredulous. But remember Mary's history. She had had seven demons cast out of her (Luke 8:2), and she who is forgiven much will love much (see the story of another woman and its conclusion in Luke 7:36–50). Mary stayed longest at the cross on the afternoon of the crucifixion. She followed Joseph and Nicodemus and watched the burial. She went to buy the spices at the close of the Sabbath. On Sunday morning, she arrived at the tomb earliest and stayed the longest.

I believe that of all the various human loves that Jesus experienced in His earthly days, that of Mary was the purest. He chose her for this high privilege: the first resurrection appearance. He also allowed the women, with their great love, to see the angels. They had a greater propensity for faith. The men expressed unbelief, but the women believed. Jesus knows who loves Him, and He measures the quality of our belief.

Yet how did He know about Mary's faithfulness through His "death days"? How did He know where she was and when she arrived at the tomb? We have seen that Jesus shares omniscience with His Father and the Spirit. He knows and He cares about intense love for Himself. Jesus knows where His disciples are.

The Appearance to the Women

Meanwhile, the other women did not know what to do after the men did not believe them. Discussing it among themselves, they decided the only reasonable thing to do was to go back to the tomb and reinvestigate the empty graveclothes.[25] As they went, Jesus now came to them. Suddenly standing before them, He stopped them and "greeted them" (Matt. 28:9) Whatever the Aramaic may have been, the Greek translates it with the imperative of *chairo*, a term that implies and imparts joy.[26]

Like Mary, these women were overwhelmed and terrified. Jesus' first task was to encourage them. He reassured them, "Do not be afraid." They seized Him by the feet, which He allowed this time for His own reasons. Matthew tells us that they "worshiped Him" (v. 9), and He graciously granted this appropriate and timely privilege. He then commanded, "Go and take word to My brethren to leave for Galilee, and there they shall see Me" (v. 10). The angels also had been told to command this trip to Galilee.

Cleopas and His Companion

Certain textual evidences (Luke 24:18, 24) indicate that word of the empty tomb was now spreading across Jerusalem. Later that day, two of the small band of twenty-three were on their way back to the village of Emmaus, about seven miles from Jerusalem. We know the name of only one of the two, Cleopas. They had left the little group after the first report of the women but before Mary's startling announcement that she had actually seen Jesus Himself. Obviously they were discussing what everybody in Jerusalem was now discussing—the crucifixion, the unbelievable miracles of nature over the weekend, and the report of the empty tomb.

Jesus now approached these two on the road, but He did something He had not done with any of the women—He held their eyes so that they would not recognize Him. The word used is a strong word (*krateo*), indicating that God "laid hold of" their perceptual apparatus.[27] In the Old Testament, when Elisha's servant was frightened by the Aramean army that surrounded Elisha, Elisha prayed and God "opened" the servant's eyes to see the Lord's chariots of fire surrounding them (2 Kings 6:17). Later the Lord caused that Aramean army to hear chariots and horses that did not exist (2 Kings 7:6). God does operate on our perceptual apparatus as it suits His purposes.

He always has a wise and valid reason for whatever He does. When Jesus appeared to Mary, she went to pieces. When He appeared to the women, they also were frightened beyond speech. Sooner or later He must be able to linger long enough to communicate the significance of these events. In other words, He must be able to talk to somebody. And so they did not recognize Him.

Jesus interrupted Cleopas and his companion: "What are these words that you are exchanging with one another as you are walking?" (Luke 24:17). Luke tells us that "they stood still, looking sad" (v. 17), frozen in their tracks to think that any pilgrim or native had escaped hearing of the cataclysmic and epochal events of the past few days. Cleopas ventured incredulously, "Are You the only one visiting Jerusalem and unaware of the things which have happened here in these days?" (v. 18).

Jesus probed for Cleopas to go on. He asked, "What things?" In wonder, Cleopas recounted the unparalleled events of the days just past, including the reported empty tomb. He added significantly, "And some of those who were with us went to the tomb and found it just exactly as the women also had said; but Him they did not see" (v. 24)—indicating several pilgrimages to gape at the empty tomb.

Jesus chided, "O foolish men and slow of heart to believe in all that the prophets have spoken!" (v. 25). Unbelief is a serious affront to Jesus. Throughout His ministry, He had repeatedly rebuked the disciples for their "little faith" (see chapters 4 and 5). Unbelief played a major part in the failure of the disciples throughout the painful struggle of this weekend and may partially account for the fact that Jesus chose not to appear to them first.

Then, "beginning with Moses and with all the prophets, He explained to them the things concerning Himself in all the Scriptures" (Luke 24:27). I have tried to imagine what wonderful Scriptures Jesus drew on during this exciting seven-mile walk. Try to fathom what it was like to hear Jesus explain the centuries-long process of the revelation of His own incarnation and sacrifice. Surely it was electrifying; later the two companions asked, "Were not our hearts burning within us while He was speaking to us on the road, while He was explaining the Scriptures to us?" (v. 32).

When they reached Emmaus after this breathtaking explanation of Old Testament Scripture, Jesus acted as though He would keep going. But they "urged Him" to come in, and Jesus always comes in where He is invited. As a good host, Cleopas spread a meal, and then, as a devout Jew, he prepared to say a blessing over it.

Suddenly, a strange thing happened. Jesus Himself took the bread, as though He owned the place and were Himself the host. He expressed thanks for it and extended it to the two companions. In that moment— probably seeing the wounds in His wrists—their eyes were opened. Suddenly they became conscious that this insightful man was Jesus Himself. But the moment they recognized Him, He was no longer there. His place at table was suddenly empty. The initial work of His first explanation to His followers was now complete, and He was gone.

Once again, note that Jesus knew which road Cleopas and his companion were on. He knew what was on their hearts. He is omniscient. He knows and He cares. The mind of Christ is a caring mind.

Would you expect them to lie down and go to sleep after such a remarkable afternoon of grasping the reality of fulfilled prophecy followed by this startling ending? In their impassioned, burning state they wanted to report as rapidly as possibly to the disciples. But would the disciples believe them? The disciples had refused to believe the report of the women about the angels. They found the disciples assembled together, a clue that something had changed in the disciples' frame of mind.

Instead of rejecting their story, the disciples affirmed its truth immediately and then revealed the cause of their assembly. They informed the two companions, "The Lord has really risen, and has appeared to Simon" (Luke 24:34). The appearance to Simon (also mentioned in 1 Cor. 15:5) is another part of the story I am unable to describe. Nothing is recorded of the special, private resurrection appearance to Simon to restore him to a relationship with Jesus after his denial. Although full restoration to ministry came in John 21, Jesus surely restored Simon to fellowship in this first appearance to him.

It must have been the most poignant memory of Peter's life—so profound, so moving, that he was unable to describe it even to his attendant, the young Mark (1 Pet. 5:13), for it does not appear in Mark's Gospel. Neither does any description of His appearance to convince His disbelieving half-brother James (1 Cor. 15:7) appear in any Gospel.

The Appearance to the Disciples

"When therefore it was evening, on that day, the first day of the week, . . . the doors were shut where the disciples were" (John 20:19). Although they now knew that the resurrection was indeed a fact, perhaps not to be understood, but at least no longer to be disputed, the disciples were still frightened. In their fear, they had locked the doors. They could not now reject Cleopas's story as summarily as they had the women's story. The miracles they had observed for three years were not exhausted after all. Somehow, incomprehensibly, some way, Jesus was alive. But why had He not appeared to the larger group of His own disciples?

Suddenly, while they were nervously trying to talk their way through these strange events, they were electrified by a new presence in their midst. Before their amazed and wondering eyes, Jesus Himself stood among them. They were stunned, for Jesus had to calm them down. He said to them, "Peace be with you" (John 20:19).

But peace did not come easily to this terrified little band. When visible proof was finally offered, they could not assimilate the reality. In spite of Peter's word, they thought they were seeing a spectral apparition and were "startled and frightened" (Luke 24:37). To allay their trembling and their fears, the Lord said, "Why are you troubled, and why do doubts arise in your hearts? See My hands and My feet, that it is I Myself; touch Me and see, for a spirit does not have flesh and bones as you see that I have" (vv. 38–39).

Previously Jesus had referred to human beings as "flesh and blood" (Matt. 16:17), but now He says that He has "flesh and bones." In our earthly bodies, the life is in the blood (Lev. 17:11). Is there a new life principle in the new body that we do not yet understand? Jesus' resurrection body in some ways was different from His previous body. The resurrection body was able to come out of a sealed tomb and to enter this locked room. Yet it also bore a resemblance to any tangible body; it could be touched and clasped. He even retained the scars of the nails in His hands and feet (as badges of honor?). The resurrection body is "flesh and bones" whatever else its properties may be.

In spite of this physical touch, the disciples remained overwhelmed and "still could not believe it for joy and were marveling." To calm their spirits further, Jesus now asked a most unexpected question: "Have you anything here to eat?" (Luke 24:41). Another property of the resurrection body is that it can eat. Hardly daring to disobey under such extraordinary circumstances, they set before Him a piece of broiled fish. To their astonishment, He "ate it before them" (v. 43). His body was not ghostly, but corporeal. He really was alive! They had even touched Him, and He was proving His substantiality by eating.

After He had demonstrated the reality of His body, Jesus issued an assurance that the disciples could now accept. In the stately solemnity of His gracious poise, He once again bestowed His serenity on the group: "Peace be with you" (John 20:21). And at last it was. Jesus' peace descended on this amazed little group. As unfathomable as it was, they accepted the resurrection as fact. What to all men in all times had been inconceivable had occurred in their own experience. This awe-struck little band of disciples finally began to take in, at least partially, the vast significance of these momentous events.

For some yet incomprehensible reason, God Himself had taken into His nature flesh and had walked on earth with them. Although they had seen the miracles, they had only vaguely appreciated their awesome, cosmic source. He had let them kill Him and had actually conquered death itself. This thing had really happened. They were in the actual presence of God incarnate.

The Lord then announced, "As the Father has sent Me, I also send you" (v. 21). With this declaration, the disciples became apostles. I never read what happened next without remembering Genesis 2:7: "Then the LORD God formed man of dust from the ground, and breathed into his nostrils the breath of life; and man became a living being." John tells us that now Jesus breathed on the disciples and said, "Receive the Holy Spirit" (John 20:22). Pentecost was now possible because of the breath of God.

Proof for Thomas

Thomas missed that meeting. Perhaps he had not heard Peter's testimony. When the excited disciples shared their overwhelming experience, Thomas could not take it in. Thomas had been loyal to the Lord when, after Jesus' announcement that Lazarus was dead, he said, "Let us also go [to Bethany], that we may die with Him" (John 11:16). The Judeans had never followed the Lord, and Thomas expected to be stoned. Later Thomas was perplexed when Jesus told the disciples that they knew the way to the place where He was going. He protested, "Lord, we do not know where You are going, how do we know the way?" (John 14:5).

Evidently the disciples told Thomas about the corporeality of Jesus' body and the demonstration of His wounds, for Thomas objected, "Unless I shall see in His hands the imprint of the nails, and put my finger into the place of the nails, and put my hand into His side, I will not believe" (John 20:25). Thomas's unbelief was consistent with his earlier pessimism, but like the unbelief of the disciples, it was tragic.

Have you ever wondered why the disciples did not immediately proceed to Galilee according to the instructions of the angel and of Jesus? They lingered in Jerusalem for a whole week. Why? They were beginning to think like Jesus thinks. The family was not yet complete; Thomas was holding out. Evidently he refused to travel to Galilee, and so they simply waited. They were beginning to have the mind of Christ.

The next Sunday night the disciples were assembled again, and Thomas was with them. Again the doors were locked, but Jesus came and once again stood in their midst. He pronounced His peace again and then ordered Thomas, "Reach here your finger, and see My hands; and reach here your hand, and put it into My side" (v. 27). How did He know what Thomas had said? Time and again, Jesus demonstrated to the disciples that He knew and cared about the quality of their faith. He then commanded Thomas, "Be not unbelieving, but believing" (v. 27).

Try to place yourself in Thomas's position at this moment. He had demanded empirical proof; now it stood before him. As stern as was

Jesus' demand for faith, He graciously granted Thomas what he needed. Thomas acquiesced totally; he yielded to the now obvious deity of Jesus and cried, "My Lord and my God!" (v. 28). Jesus told him, "Because you have seen Me, have you believed? Blessed are they who did not see, and yet believed" (v. 29).

The Command to Peter

Now began the eighty-mile walk to Galilee, a distance that required two days of hard walking and more if the walk were done leisurely. The angel and Jesus had spoken of this important appearance in Galilee. This appearance was to be the only one by appointment: the disciples were told the place to expect Him. The meeting was not to be secret like the other meetings. As word spread among those who had remained loyal to the Lord after the masses deserted in John 6, excitement grew in anticipation of the time.

One day, while they were waiting, Peter decided to go fishing. He was joined by Thomas, Nathanael (Bartholomew?), James, John, and two others. Normally net fishing is done at night in Galilee. Fish come to the surface during the cool of the evening. The next morning, as they prepared to end a fruitless night, they saw a figure on the shore. Naturally the villagers came to the incoming boats to buy fish. The man on the shore called out, "Children, you do not have any fish, do you?" (John 21:5). When they confirmed His negative question, he told them, "Cast the net on the right-hand side of the boat, and you will find a catch" (v. 6). This was a strange directive, because after daylight the fish would normally go to deeper water, but the disciples obeyed. Suddenly the net was so full it nearly broke.

This had happened before! (See Luke 5:4–7.) John, always so quick to perceive, exclaimed to Peter, "It is the Lord" (John 21:7). Peter impulsively swam to the shore. When the disciples landed, they found that Jesus indeed had come once again and had cooked breakfast for them.

After breakfast, Jesus asked Peter, "Simon, son of John, do you love Me more than these?" (v. 15). Simon had been quick to claim his loyalty when Jesus predicted that he would deny Him (Matt. 26:35), yet he denied his Lord. He now responded, "Yes, Lord; You know that I love You." Jesus told him, "Tend My lambs" (v. 15). Jesus then repeated the question, and Peter once again affirmed his love. Jesus told him, "Shepherd My sheep" (v. 16). Jesus asked a third time, and Peter protested, "Lord, You know all things"—and He does—"You know that

I love You." And Jesus once again commanded, "Tend My sheep" (v. 17). He entrusted to Simon Peter the care of His most precious possession on earth—His own sheep.

The Great Commission
The day finally arrived for the great meeting for which the angel and Jesus had prepared them. This one appearance by appointment was to be on a mountain, and more than five hundred persons were there. Excitement must have been at a fever pitch while they awaited His coming. Among the crowd were loyal followers and some who possibly came out of curiosity and could not actually accept the reality of a resurrection from the dead.

Suddenly Jesus came. Reverence fell over the multitude and the true believers worshiped Him. With His followers and His disciples alert and intense, He gave a monumental commission: "All authority has been given to Me in heaven and on earth. Go therefore and make disciples of all the nations, baptizing them in the name of the Father and the Son and the Holy Spirit, teaching them to observe all that I commanded you; and lo, I am with you always, even to the end of the age" (Matt. 28:18–20).

The message of Christ was now enlarged to include the whole world. The disciples did not comprehend all that He had said until later (Acts 10). Significantly, He spoke these words to the large crowd. Christians of all ages are grateful that He assured them of His continuing presence. He had known and understood the state of mind of Mary Magdalene and of Cleopas and his companion. He had been there when Thomas spoke his unbelieving words. He is with us even today.

Other Appearances
After the Great Commission, Jesus sent the little band of disciples back to Jerusalem for the next part of His massive plan. In Jerusalem, He came again to tell them, "All things which are written about Me in the Law of Moses and the Prophets and the Psalms must be fulfilled" (Luke 24:44). Once again, we find the Lord Himself explaining Scripture to His followers. The conceptual is important, for He now "opened their minds" (v. 45). He told them: "Thus it is written, that the Christ should suffer and rise again from the dead the third day; and that repentance for forgiveness of sins should be proclaimed in His name to all the nations, beginning from Jerusalem. You are witnesses of these things. And behold, I am sending forth the promise of My Father upon you; but

you are to stay in the city until you are clothed with power from on high" (Luke 24:46–49).

On what may have been another occasion, Jesus shared a meal with the little band. At that moment He commanded them not to leave Jerusalem but to wait for what the Father had promised, "Which . . . you heard of from Me; for John baptized with water, but you shall be baptized with the Holy Spirit not many days from now" (Acts 1:4–5).

The Ascension

Many people over the centuries have tried to attribute these appearances of the risen Christ to hallucinations. But hallucinations only occur with certain types of people. Jesus appeared to all kinds—to individual women and men, to small groups and to large groups. Hallucinations, for people who have them, normally happen at the same time of day. But Jesus appeared in the early morning, through the course of the day, and at night. Hallucinations do not suddenly stop.[28] But Jesus Christ enacted a distinct farewell.

He led the disciples to the Mount of Olives in the vicinity of Bethany, west of Jerusalem. They asked, "Lord, is it at this time You are restoring the kingdom to Israel?" (Acts 1:6). He answered, "It is not for you to know times or epochs which the Father has fixed by His own authority" (v. 7). Once again He tried to enlarge their consciousness of His commission: "But you shall receive power when the Holy Spirit has come upon you; and you shall be My witnesses both in Jerusalem, and in all Judea and Samaria, and even to the remotest part of the earth" (v. 8).

For His final act, He lifted His hands and blessed His own followers. Then, before their eyes, He began to leave the earth and to ascend to heaven. In view of all they had been through, this was no longer so abnormal, so unexpected. Even in His years of ministry, they had seen Him walk on water.

But what happened next had tremendous significance for any true Hebrew. Throughout the Bible, clouds are associated with the exclusive glory of God. Later Jews and Christians would call it the "Shekinah," the visible expression of the divine presence, especially when resting between the cherubim over the mercy seat in the Holy of Holies. The glory cloud had led Israel out of Egypt (Exod. 13:21). As it stood between Egypt and Israel, "there was the cloud along with the darkness, yet it gave light at night" (Exod. 14:20). As Moses spoke to the Israelite community, "they looked toward the wilderness, and behold, the glory of the LORD appeared in the cloud" (Exod. 16:10). The glory cloud appeared when the tabernacle was dedicated (Exod. 40:34) and later "the glory" (obviously a cloud) appeared when the temple was dedicated (2 Chron. 7:1–3). Later even Isaiah saw it (Isa. 6:4).

Then Israel went eight hundred years without the visible manifestation of God's glory, until one day Jesus led three of His disciples up a mountain, and these three (Peter, James, and John) saw the Shekinah (Matt. 17:5). Still, eight of the disciples had never seen it.

Suddenly, before the amazed eyes of the disciples, a cloud appeared. It abruptly hid Jesus from their sight. Any true Hebrew would immediately grasp the significance of that phenomenon. The glory cloud signified the presence of God Himself. The cloud rose and disappeared into heaven, out of their sight.

Elijah had ascended into heaven in a whirlwind (2 Kings 2:11). He needed to be transported. But when Jesus ascended into heaven, He did not need a taxi; He knew the way. Only Jesus could appropriately ascend on the glory cloud that signifies the presence of God. He was seated at the right hand of God the Father (Acts 2:33), where He began the new and important work of intercession for His disciples on earth (Heb. 7:25).

Two angels suddenly confronted the disciples, who lingered and were gaping at the now empty sky. They challenged the men, "Men of Galilee, why do you stand looking into the sky? This Jesus, who has been taken up from you into heaven, will come *in just the same way* as you have watched Him go into heaven" (Acts 1:11, emphasis added). Luke tells us that "they returned to Jerusalem with great joy, and were continually in the temple, praising God" (24:52–53).

A time is approaching when believers will desperately need hope, and believers on earth at that time once again will be privileged at last to see the Shekinah. "And then will they see the Son of Man coming in a cloud with power and great glory. But when these things begin to take place, straighten up and lift up your heads, because your redemption is drawing near" (Luke 21:27–28).

The Resurrection Changes Lives

The cross changes lives because it changes our nature. The resurrection changes lives because it changes our outlook. The world was changed two thousand years ago because the outlook of the disciples changed.

Their outlook after Christ's death was one of pessimism and gloom. The high optimism of the years of Christ's ministry was dashed, and all confidence disappeared. At that point all they could make of the crucifixion was the horrible fact of death. They huddled behind locked doors and refused to believe the report of the women who had seen the angels (Luke 24:11).

Their outlook changed abruptly. They saw the risen Christ and watched Him ascend. The cowardly fear that made them lock their doors was transformed into a courage that defied the Sanhedrin (Acts 4:8–20). Men who had considered Christ's death a defeat were changed into fiery evangelists who spread the gospel from Jerusalem to Judea, to Samaria, and to "the remotest part of the earth." The otherwise inexplicable change in these men is one undeniable proof of the reality of the resurrection.

Although we cannot physically see the risen Christ as the disciples did, we can experience the power of His resurrection. The history of Christianity is a story of martyrs who so knew that power that they gave their lives for the gospel. It is a story of statesmen who stood strong for the faith when it was not politically expedient. It tells about missionaries who left home and comfort to penetrate the dangers of savagery and cannibalism with the gospel. These courageous persons had their outlook changed.

Strange to say, we know the power of the resurrection by identifying with Christ in His death. Paul said he was crucified with Christ (Gal. 2:20). I experienced death to my self in 1959 (see chapter 5). Paul said that we experience the power of the resurrection by becoming like Christ in His death (Phil. 3:10). In the next verse, he said that he would be resurrected because he shared in Christ's death.

The only place resurrection can occur is out of death. What do you need to die to? For me it was a career. For some it is money and comfort. For others it may be an inordinate affection. In prayer, give it to God. He knows how to bring new life where we would not expect it.

Conclusion

The greatest battle in the history of the universe was the struggle over the human life of Jesus. Because He defeated Satan, I live in victory. Death has no more sting in my mind. Life may be a struggle, but the outcome is assured. Ungodly fear is inappropriate for me. My victory is not really my own, but the victory of the Lion of the Tribe of Judah.

PART THREE

A Name
Above Every Name

chapter eleven

A Kingdom Above

hath given him a name above every name

The ascension of Christ did not consist merely of the lifting of His physical body upward, out of this realm and into another. It symbolized His exaltation above all of creation. He was seated at the right hand of the Father (Eph. 1:20) to undertake the work of intercession for His followers (Heb. 7:25). Being at the right hand of God tells us that He is above all of us. Paul says He is "far above all rule and authority and power and dominion, and every name that is named, not only in this age, but also in the one to come. And [God] put all things in subjection under His feet" (Eph. 1:21–22).

Jesus told His disciples, "My Father has granted Me a kingdom" (Luke 22:29). Later He said to Pilate, "My kingdom is not of this world" (John 18:36). For the present, Christ's kingdom is above and is spiritual in nature. Believers are the subjects in that kingdom (Col. 1:13).

Christ existed before His own creation (Col. 1:17). Since He brought it into being, all of it is under Him. The unregenerate, however, cannot acknowledge His lordship because they do not know Him. Although He is in control of their circumstances and their lives, they are unaware of His beneficence (Matt. 5:45).

Therefore we who are His subjects must treat Him as the sovereign that He is. He must have preeminence among His own people. "He is the head of the body, the church; and He is the beginning, the first-born from the dead, so that He Himself might come to have first place in everything" (Col. 1:18).

Is Christ absolute lord of your life? When I acknowledged His lordship in 1959, it meant that I would submit to His sovereignty in every area of my life. He is Lord of my marriage, my friendships, my business, my leisure, even of my checkbook. His lordship also means that I will obey as He directs my life.

Our hymn declares that every knee will bow at the name of Jesus, "of those who are in heaven, and on earth, and under the earth" (Phil 2:10). Whatever these phrases mean, they surely include all of creation. We will all bow to Christ and confess His lordship over our lives (v. 11).

If we are all going to do that ultimately, would it not be intelligent to get ahead of the crowd and do it now? Significantly, every time the phrase "Lord and Savior" occurs (always in 2 Peter), the word "Lord" precedes the word "Savior" (1:11, 2:20, 3:18). This is the way the early church thought. The emphasis was on lordship.

I urge you at this point in reading this book to acknowledge His lordship in all of your life if you have not already done that. Make it a conscious act of your will so that you will remember this specific event.

It is at the name of Jesus that we will bow. His names tell us much about Him and about our relationship to Him.

The Names of Christ

One of the ways we relate to one another is through our names. I have many names and all of them in one way or another signify relationships. My name is "T.W.," "Honey," "Doc," "Brother," and "Prof," to name a few. I can tell what kind of mood my wife is in by the name she uses for me.

Several years ago I got a new name as my grandchildren came along: "Papa" (pronounced "Paw-paw"). That is what they call me most of the time. Sometimes when they want my attention quickly, they will address me as "Dr. Hunt." Then occasionally when they want to show affection (or when they want something), they call me "Pops."

Now I respond strongly to these names (especially "Pops"). Why do I do that? Because I am a person, and names indicate personal relationships. Christ also is a person, and He responds when we use His various names. His names are as important to Him as yours are to you.

Just as you would relate to me by using one of my several names, you can relate to Christ, even though He is divine, by becoming familiar with and using His revealed names. You can witness about Him by using such names as "Savior," "Redeemer," and even "Friend." You can share with fellow believers such names as "Brother" and "Everlasting Father." Names meaningful to troubled people are "Wonderful Counselor" and "Prince of Peace." The names are useful to bring us immediately into His presence.

Because He is preeminent, we enter His presence reverently. I try to use the names with circumspection and thoughtfulness. Christ is infinitely above us. Even His names inform us of His exalted station.

A single chapter cannot introduce you to all the names of Christ. Therefore, let me extract ten principles that organize some of the names. The principles below are not mutually exclusive; some names could be included under several principles.

The Complement Principle

One aspect of our submission to Christ is to fulfill a complementary role that His names suggest. If He is Shepherd (John 10:11), then I am a sheep. As Shepherd, He is Guardian, and requires of me growth and reproduction. He is a Father (Isa. 9:6), and so I am a child. As Father, He is provider and wants of me a relationship. The complement of Brother (Heb. 2:11) is brother or sister, and He expects resemblance of me. He is Teacher (John 3:2), and so I am a disciple. As Teacher, He Himself is the information I am to assimilate, and He expects me to learn of Him. I must learn His attributes, His ways, His mind, and His life. He is the Leader (Isa. 55:4), and so I am a follower. As Leader, He guides me, and expects me to know His steps.

He is the Master (2 Tim. 2:21), and so I must be a servant. He, therefore, does the planning, and my job is obedience. To do that, I must acknowledge His authority. This, I believe, is why the disciples were chosen; they recognized His authority and always obeyed Him immediately. He is the Vine (John 15:5), and I am a branch. As Vine, He is my Source, and my responsibility is abiding. Fruit is not a work, but a result of abiding. He is the Bridegroom (Mark 2:19), and we, His church, constitute the Bride of Christ. As Bridegroom, He is our Lover and expects faithfulness of us.

The Identity Principle

When we apply the Identity Principle, we identify with Christ in certain of His names, that is, we are to grow into His likeness in certain specific ways. Because of our redemption, we first identify with Him in His position. For example, He is the Beloved (Matt. 12:18). If we are in Christ, we must be also beloved by God. Paul wrote the saints in Rome that they were "beloved of God" (Rom. 1:7). He is the Chosen One (Isa. 42:1), and we also are chosen (2 Tim. 2:10). He is the Heir of All Things (Heb. 1:2), but wonder of wonders, we are fellow heirs with Him (Rom. 8:17). What is our position? We are seated with Christ in the heavenly realms (Eph. 2:6); we are hidden with Christ in God (Col. 3:3).

We also identify with Christ in His humanity. He is the Last Adam (1 Cor. 15:45). Even though He is illimitable, He became local. He is the Nazarene (Matt. 2:23). The people who live below His standard are really subhuman. Our power of life-changing decision means that we are not limited to our animal nature. We may never excuse our sins by saying that we are "only" human. Christ, as the Last Adam, showed us what God's ideal for humanity is. The ideal human is profoundly spiritual.

We identify with Him in His character. He is a Lamb (John 1:29), which is to say He is pure. Only in Christ are we pure, but if He is in us, we have His character. He is a Rock (1 Cor. 10:4), and in Him we do not waver. He is Jesus Christ the Righteous (1 John 2:1), and in Him I am righteous (Jer. 23:6).

We identify with Him in His joy. He is the Blessed (Ps. 72:17), as I am if I am in Him. He is "Christ in you, the Hope of Glory" (Col. 1:27). This word for "you" in this verse is plural, so we can only realize that hope in the context of the Body of Christ. He is the Desired of All Nations (Hag. 2:7 KJV). If you become like Christ, do not be surprised if people are drawn to you. But also remember that many types of people in this world will respond to you in the same way that they did to Christ. Jesus said, "If the world hates you, you know that it has hated Me before it hated you. . . . If they persecuted Me, they will also persecute you; if they kept My word, they will keep yours also" (John 15:18, 20).

Another point of identification is in His authority. Jesus is the Anointed (Ps. 2:2). Since He is in me, my anointing is His indwelling. If He is in me, then the power and wisdom of God dwell in my person (1 Cor. 1:24).

The Response Principle

Certain of His names were given for us to respond to Him. In each of these names, God is proffering us Christ as a Gift. If I bow the knee, then I will seek and make appropriate response to each of these names.

To the Samaritan woman, Jesus referred to Himself as the Gift of God (John 4:10). The implication of this gift name is that God has shown us favor; our response is receiving. Jesus is the Resurrection (John 11:25). The implication is death; the only place resurrection occurs is in a graveyard. Our response is in living for Him. In Christ, God gives us the Bread of Life (John 6:35). The implication is that God will sustain us; our appropriation is in feeding on Him. The implication of His name as Door or Gate (John 10:7) is choice. We choose God by choosing Christ and enter God's presence only through Him. He is our Friend (John 15:15) and in assuming that name, He is indicating that He would like to be in our company. To bow the knee to Him, I must respond to this group of His names.

The Functioning Names

These names indicate some way in which Jesus works for us or functions on our behalf. He is the Angel of His Presence (who saved His people; see Isa. 63:9). I can count on the presence of God, because that is Jesus' name. He is with me. As the Man of Sorrows (Isa. 53:3), He bore my griefs. He is the Savior of the World (John 4:42), and I am one of His world whom He saved. He is the Shepherd and Guardian of our Souls (1 Pet. 2:25), and so I know He will watch over and care for me. God displayed Him publicly as the Propitiation in His Blood (Rom. 3:25), and so I know that my sin debt is fully paid. We bow the knee to these names when we accept Christ as our Savior; we remain in submission when we continually trust and rest in the adequacy of His work. Some of these names could be called redemption names.

The Life Principle

Certain names for the Lord indicate that He is the source of our life. Whenever a name is repeated in various permutations, God is emphasizing the importance of the concept back of that name. Thomas asked Him the way He was going, and Jesus told Thomas, "I am the way, and the truth, and the life" (John 14:6). Only in Christ can we have a full life. He said, "I came that they might have life, and might have it abundantly" (John 10:10). Peter's name for Him is Prince of Life (Acts 3:15). First John 1:2 even calls Him "Eternal Life." He is the life-giving Spirit (1 Cor. 15:45). On the occasion of raising Lazarus from the dead, He called Himself the Resurrection and the Life (John 11:25).

The Light Names

John says that Jesus is the True Light (John 1:9). Jesus Himself claimed to be the Light of the World (John 8:12). The Bible talks about the people of this world as Jews and Gentiles. For the Jews, Jesus is the Star out of Jacob (Num. 24:17 KJV); for the Gentiles, He is the Light of Revelation to the Gentiles (Luke 2:32). Small wonder then that John says He is the Light of Men (John 1:4).

But He is also the Light of Heaven. Zechariah's song called Him the Sunrise from on High, or the Dawn who will "shine upon those who sit in darkness and the shadow of death" (Luke 1:79). Significantly, in Jesus' last word in the New Testament, He called Himself the Bright Morning Star (Rev. 22:16). This name—His last word to us—signifies hope. In the Day of the Lord, He will be the Sun of Righteousness (Mal. 4:2). In the New Jerusalem, "the city has no need of the sun or of the moon to shine upon it, for the glory of God has illumined it, and its lamp is the Lamb" (Rev. 21:23). Note that you have to look up in the sky to see all these manifestations of light. These are celestial, or heavenly, light names.

Paul wrote Timothy that God dwells in "unapproachable light" (1 Tim. 6:16). Yet Jesus Himself is the Radiance of God's Glory (Heb. 1:3), and He is our access to God. Whether we need enlightenment or illumination for our path, Jesus is the True Light.

The Sovereign Principle

Many names indicate the sovereignty of Christ. Daniel's name for Him is Messiah the Prince (Dan. 9:25). He is the Prince and Savior in Acts 5:31 and the Prince of Peace in Isaiah 9:6. Micah's prophecy calls Him the Ruler in Israel (Mic. 5:2).

We have already seen that His name is Lord. That name is used sixty-four times in the Gospels and Acts, and so His authority and dominion were assumed in the earliest days of His ministry and of the church. Even His half-brother Jude said He was Master and Lord (v. 4). Since He is the supreme ruler, He would obviously be a King (Isa. 32:1). Zechariah calls Him the King over All the Earth (14:9), and the psalmist says He is the King of Glory (Ps. 24:10). Ultimately He will be shown to be the Lord of lords and King of kings (Rev. 17:14).

The Preeminence Principle

We have already seen that He is to be preeminent in all things. Paul calls Him the firstborn among many brethren (Rom. 8:29) and the firstborn of all creation (Col. 1:15). Paul also places Him as the head of every man (1 Cor. 11:3) and the head over all things to the church (Eph. 1:22). Isaiah heard God say that He is the leader and commander for the peoples (55:4). Perhaps the most important of the preeminence names is Paul's designation, "Lord of All" (Rom. 10:12).

These verses show that Paul expected Christ to be supreme in the New Testament church and in the lives of believers. If we are going to bow the knee today, we will place Christ above all earthly relations, institutions, pastimes, and businesses.

The Deity Names

Inevitably we expect to find a number of designations of Christ as divine. Peter told the onlookers in the temple that He was the Holy and Righteous One (Acts 3:14). Paul indicated His origin when he said Jesus was the Man from Heaven (1 Cor. 15:47). Paul also said He was the Image of the Invisible God (Col. 1:15), and the writer of Hebrews said He was the Exact Representation of God's Nature (Heb. 1:3). He is that because He is the Son of the Blessed One (Mark 14:61), which is to say, the Son of God. Isaiah's prophecy called Him the Mighty God (9:6). God had the angel instruct Joseph to name Him Immanuel, according to the prophecy in Isaiah 7:14, which means, "God with us" (Matt. 1:23). God's grace gave us Immanuel.

Perhaps the most important of the divine names is Jesus' own claim to be the I Am (John 8:58), in this way connecting Himself with the eternal self-existent God who appeared to Moses (Exod. 3:14). He is one with the other members of the Trinity. The Father, the Son, and the Spirit are eternal.

The Alpha and Omega Principle

I use this designation for this series of names because it is biblical, a name Christ gave Himself, and expresses so well the idea contained in the principle. Alpha is the first letter of the Greek alphabet; Omega is the last. We would say the A and the Z. Some of the Alpha names indicate Christ as initiator. All initiative is with God. The Omega names, on the other hand, indicate Him as a finisher. God always finishes what He starts. After Jesus said, "I am the Alpha and the Omega," He emphasized it by adding "the first and the last, the beginning and the end" (Rev. 22:13). He is the Author (initiator) and the Perfecter of Faith (Heb. 12:2).

He is the Advocate with the Father (1 John 2:1). One of the technical meanings of this word was "defense lawyer." This is an Alpha name. I need not fear the constant accusation of Satan (Rev. 12:10), for He who initiated my salvation constantly stands ready to defend me. But not only is He the Alpha, He also has a corresponding Omega name—"Judge" (Acts 10:42). What an unbeatable combination; our defense lawyer is our judge. Jesus begins and finishes the work on my behalf.

As Alpha, He is the Lamb who took away our sins (John 1:29). As Lamb, He is meek, pure, and innocent. But as Omega, he is the Lion That Is from the Tribe of Judah (Rev. 5:5). As Lion, He is bold and will conquer in the end. Jesus is both Lamb and Lion, Alpha and Omega.

One of His Alpha names is Servant (Acts 4:30). As Servant, He submits to God and even assumed a role among the disciples as "One Who Serves" (Luke 22:27). But Jesus is also the Omega; as Omega, He is the Head of the Church (Eph. 5:23). As Head, He directs the work of the servants.

Another Alpha name is Apostle—the Sent One who came to earth to begin a new work for all of us. But He also has a corresponding Omega name—the High Priest (Heb. 3:1) who now intercedes for us. He is the Son of Man (Matt. 11:19) and the Son of God (1 John 4:15).

Jesus is not only the A and the Z. He is the BCDEFGHIJKLMN-OPQRSTUVWXY! He who begins the work and finishes it also does the work through us throughout our lives (John 15:1–5). In the stages of life, He is the Child (Isa. 9:6), the Man (1 Tim. 2:5), and the Eternal Father (Isa. 9:6). In regard to the building, He is the Foundation (1 Cor. 3:11), the Cornerstone (1 Pet. 2:6), and even the Builder (Heb. 3:3). If we see Him as Plant, He is the Seed from which we all spring (Gal. 3:16), the Root (Rom. 15:12), the Branch (Zech. 6:12), and the Vine (John 15:1). As to His churchly offices, He is the Apostle (Heb. 3:1), the Prophet (Acts 3:22), the High Priest (Heb. 5:10), and the Overseer or Bishop (1 Pet. 2:25 KJV). He is the Alpha and Omega, the summation of all the work of God.

I submit to Christ in some of His names (Master, Teacher). Others help me relate to Him (Friend, Brother). Some of the names provide comfort and assurance (The Resurrection and the Life, Immanuel). I enjoy some of them (Blessed, Gift of God).

Most important of all, I use them in worship (Holy and Righteous One, Image of the Invisible God). Our word *worship*, comes from an old Anglo-Saxon word, *weorth-scipe*, which meant "worth-ship." Christ is worthy of our worship and adoration.

His Offices

The creed of the New Testament church was "Jesus Christ is Lord"—the confession of every tongue in Philippians 2:11. The confession of faith in Romans 10:9 is of "Jesus as Lord." Paul wrote the Corinthian church, "No one can say, 'Jesus is Lord,' except by the Holy Spirit" (1 Cor. 12:3). Jesus told the disciples, "You call Me Teacher and Lord; and you are right, for so I am" (John 13:13).

The three titles—Jesus, Christ, and Lord—occur in conjunction repeatedly throughout the New Testament. In his great Pentecost sermon, Peter preached, "God has made Him both Lord and Christ" (Acts 2:36). Later, Peter preached to Cornelius "peace through Jesus Christ (He is Lord of all)" (Acts 10:36). As early as his first letter to the Thessalonians, Paul greeted them in "the Lord Jesus Christ" (1:1), and his letters are sprinkled generously with references to "Christ Jesus the Lord." God's intention is for that phrase—Jesus Christ is Lord—to be the marching flag of today's New Testament church.

Jesus was the name of the incarnate God, His human name. In this human nature, He functioned as prophet (Acts 3:22), the first of His three great offices. God speaks through a prophet, and if a prophet speaks, we must listen.

The name Christ brings in and combines both His human and His divine natures. Christ is His name as priest (Heb. 4:14). The Old Testament priests had a number of observances that (we see in retrospect) were really reminders for the people. We cannot now examine the many feasts and festivals of Israel. We can say, however, that the Passover was a reminder that God acts. The Day of Atonement was a reminder of what the people owed in their sin debt. All the observances find their fulfillment in the work and sacrifice of Christ. Our priest has given us an important observance, Communion, or the Lord's Supper. This act, however, is a reminder of what has been paid.

Our great high priest now functions in two ways. First, He is an intercessor (Heb. 7:25). This word tells us where He is, between us and God. Second, He is our mediator (1 Tim. 2:5). This word tells us what He does, His work.

His third great office is that of king (Rev. 19:16). His name as king is Lord (Phil. 2:11). This name brings in the divine nature. God rules through Christ as Lord, and we bow the knee.

His three great offices, then, are contained in the formula. As a human, He was Jesus the prophet. This involves His past work. The name Christ brings in both His human and divine natures and shows Him as priest. The priestly work is His present work for us. The last name in the creed, Lord, shows Him to us as king. This speaks of a future day when every knee will bow. In this way, the creed contained every important idea in the work and nature of Christ: "Jesus (prophet) Christ (priest) is Lord (king)." It gives us His names, His major offices, and His work.

Because He is a prophet, I heed His word. He is a prophet who speaks the oracles of God, and I treasure that word. Because He is a priest, I believe Him. Since He is king, I have acknowledged His total lordship over every area of my life. Every knee will bow, and I am grateful that I've already done that.

Conclusion

Christ's name before me at all times facilitates my thinking His thoughts and demonstrating His character. Knowing His position, authority, and work, I want to worship Him. My worship can only be measured by His worth. He helps me worship in His office as Lord. God's goal is the lordship of Christ. My creed is "Jesus Christ is Lord." He rules in my heart.

chapter twelve

A Kingdom Within

hath given him a name above every name

Jesus emphasized that the kingdom of God does not come with outward observance, but rather, "the kingdom of God is within you" (Luke 17:21 KJV). That directs us to the mind, the area where God wants to work. The changes that He brings in our life are secret and inward, but these changes are likely to bear outward fruit. The outward fruit is only a visible symbol of inner change.

Jesus said, "Seek first His kingdom and His righteousness" (Matt. 6:33). Seeking the kingdom within, in our heart, must take priority. Our outward witness and our going as missionaries will be ineffective if we are not changed inwardly.

The fact that you are reading this book says that you are seeking that kingdom within. If you have tried to do and observe all that I have suggested in the various tests, exercises, and directions in this book until now, you should have seen some change. For me each of the steps I have shared so far meant a radical restructuring of my own thought life. Each new step forward has opened the path to another unexpected step. Every victory for me has meant a new test from Satan. Overcoming in one area means a new battle in another area; later we will see that God works in process.

The new way of thinking that we have been learning must be put into some sort of mental framework. The Germans gave us a useful word to describe our general outlook on life, *Weltanschauung*. It means "world-view" and refers to the comprehensive view we take of the world, our business, our spiritual life, our family life, eternity; it is our understanding of the world in which we live and the way all of it fits together. You have many pieces of a new way of thinking now, but those pieces must be a part of an overview of life or outlook that will be permanent and yet flexible enough to receive new information.

Two World-views

Any single world-view will be modified by individual circumstances, family, friends, and background. God is too creative to allow His creatures to be all of one mold. Nevertheless, most of the people of this world do tend to look at things from the vantage point of their present physical world. I have traveled all over the world many times. Always as I go, I am struck by a degree of sameness among the peoples of the world. Certain aspects of world-view remain constant, regardless of the culture.

I have also known many Christians around the world. Again, most of us have certain goals in common. The daily life both of the peoples of the world and of various kinds of Christians is marked by cultural differences and millions of individual personality inflections. However, for the present, I want to present two overarching world-views that include to one degree or another most of the people I have known. For the present, we will simply accept the fact that those two overarching views will have many inflections.

The first is the viewpoint of the world. Its author is Satan, and it is so common that we take its assumptions for granted. We will call this the worldly view. The second is the viewpoint of spiritual Christians, serving God with all their heart. We will call this the Christly world-view. As you read about these two views, you may see yourself as a spiritual Christian, yet with certain worldly assumptions intruding upon your viewpoint. Our goal is to position ourselves entirely within the Christly world-view. All of the various exercises and tests until now have assumed that the Christly world-view was necessary for the expression of the mind of Christ.

The worldly view sees most of the circumstances of our life as deriving from fortune or chance. Sometimes people with this world-view set goals, but ultimately they feel that the outcome will depend on unpredictable elements. Their world consists of likelihoods, possibilities, and probabilities. Ambition plays a major role in this outlook for some people, but the factor of accident always remains a possibility for them. They want eagerly to know the future, and some of them even consult mediums or horoscopes to get clues about the direction of their life. They may wish upon a star or count on their lucky penny or some other talisman.

If life does not turn out like they want or expect, they may become bitter and disappointed. They may feel or express gratification, but often it is momentary. They curse their luck or bless their fortune. This view rarely sees the long term.

The Christly world-view, on the other hand, sees God in control of all circumstances. It recognizes that circumstances may not turn out well immediately, but it does not blame God when they seem to turn out wrong. They derive their goals from God, and expect Him to carry them to fruition. If a given goal is not realized, they expect God to reweave the tapestry of their life to achieve something greater than they had envisioned. The steps along the way, bad or good, are an incidental part of a larger picture.

Although this view does not blame God, it does credit Him with His gracious works. People with this view know the real meaning of thanking God for all things. What might seem an ordinary happenstance in other lives becomes in their life a good that they could not have expected. They see blessing in daily food, in the oxygen we breathe, in the friends God gives us, and even in various family circumstances, favorable or unfavorable.

They are secure because they know the future rests in God's hands and He loves them. They firmly believe that all things indeed work together for ultimate good. They do not worry about the particular form of good that may take, because a loving Father is dispensing His version of the good with kind intentions.

Once I became concerned about a certain sin in my past. It happened to be a mental sin, but I knew that God knew fully the condition of my mind. I had confessed the sin but lived in fear that I might commit the sin again. I became obsessed with fear because of my past. The obsession continued to plague me for some time until I realized that uncertainty was not fitting for a spiritual Christian. I felt a need to pray through my anxiety.

As I prayed, Paul's word to the Philippians suddenly leaped to my mind: "Forgetting what lies behind and reaching forward to what lies ahead, I press on toward the goal for the prize of the upward call of God in Christ Jesus" (Phil. 3:13–14). Suddenly I realized the secret of the difference in this one aspect of the worldly view and the Christly view. The worldly view teaches that we are a product of the past; the Christly view teaches that we are a product of the future. God is moving us toward a goal.

In the humanistic world-view, we are what we have been. In the spiritual world-view, we are what we are becoming. None of that is due to chance. God's intention is that I be like Christ. To accomplish that He will use means I do not yet understand. The fact that I do not understand it does not matter, because I know God's ultimate intention. My job is not to be perfect now, but to cooperate with God and His means, whatever they turn out to be, of perfecting me.

I do not yet know the particular manifestations of Christ that will characterize what God is making of me. It does not matter. God knows. I am moving toward a goal. What matters is not what I have been, but what God is making of me. When I realized that, I began to feel secure in God's work in my life. I do not know the future, but I know God. I know that He will conform me to the image of Christ in particular ways so that Christ will be glorified and my service for Him will be complete. By the way, that particular mental sin has not bothered me since I deliberately placed it in the perspective of the Christly world-view. My job is to forget the past and press forward. Can you do that?

The worldly view ultimately touches the physical. The important matters of life can be measured by some physical limit: sex, food, money, or position. Since it is measurable, the worldly view relies on proof. The proof must somehow satisfy a tangible measure. The flesh wants validation of its own worth.

The Christly world-view is basically spiritual. It sees all of life in terms of unseen values. Several years ago I became aware that Jesus always saw aspects and factors other people did not see. If they were in a storm, the disciples saw winds and waves, but Jesus saw the controlling hand of God. If they were in a crowd, the disciples saw the thronging multitude, but Jesus saw a sick woman who needed ministry. At the time I cried out to the Lord, "Lord, how can I see life as Jesus saw it?"

I determined to start trying to find ways to say to God, "I believe the spiritual is greater than the physical and has control over the physical." For example, one can see what is important to a person by his checkbook. I examined my own checkbook to see what values my purchases and payments had reflected. Fasting also says to God, "I believe my body is subject to my spirit." (People with certain health conditions should not fast; consult your doctor before fasting.)

One night as I started out of church, a friend of mine, a singer, stopped me and asked that I pray for her sleep. She said she had not been able to sleep lately. I prayed right there for her sleep. When I got home, it suddenly struck me that this was yet another way to tell God that I valued the spiritual above the physical. I decided to sacrifice my own sleep for my friend's.

I began by praying for her brain waves. I asked God to make her brain waves relax and settle down to an alpha level. As I continued to pray, I became concerned that she breathe deeply in her sleep. I asked God to send fresh supplies of oxygen to refresh the tired cells in her body. I continued in this vein until about 4:00 A.M.

I began praying for her brain waves to quicken. I asked God to wake her up to a delicious sense of the presence of the Lord Jesus. Then I prayed that the Holy Spirit would give her the best morning prayer time she had ever had. Later someone told me that she bounced into her office the next morning full of energy. She told the office staff, "You would not believe the night of sleep T.W. prayed down on me last night. And when I woke up, I woke up thinking about the Lord Jesus. This morning God gave me the most blessed quiet time I have ever had!"

The physical is controlled by the spiritual. A spiritual God created this physical universe, and He has never relaxed His control of it. The Christly world-view relies not on sight, but on faith. It maintains a close relationship with the Holy Spirit, who knows the mind of Christ and the mind of the Father.

The physical world is important. God made it and said that it was good. Therefore we value it and we enjoy it. But it is subservient to the spiritual and serves the spiritual.

The worldly view wants satisfaction or gratification. It is subject to impulse and lives for the moment. Sometimes it is haunted by the past, but it also wants instant gratification. When the gratification is past, it begins expecting the next gratification. It cannot know a continuum of gratification.

The Christly view has joy. That joy continues day after day, month after month. Its moments of pleasure are but punctuation marks in the continuum of joy in the Holy Spirit. When trouble comes, it still remembers the first point above in the differences between the two world-views: God is in control. Paul and Silas were in prison, but they sang hymns of praise to God (Acts 16:25).

The worldly view has moments, but the Christly world-view lives in the present. In that continuum, the future invades the present with the blessing of the "hope we have as an anchor of the soul, a hope both sure and steadfast" (Heb. 6:19).

The worldly view lives from gratification to gratification, lacking specific development. The Christian, however, knows that God works in process. That process is a continuum of progress marked by joy. The stages of that progress move "from glory to glory": "But we all, with unveiled face beholding as in a mirror the glory of the Lord, are being transformed into the same image from glory to glory, just as from the Lord, the Spirit" (2 Cor. 3:18).

In Mark 4:26–29, Jesus told about the slowly growing seed. From day to day the farmer cannot see the difference in the plant, but he knows when it is ready for harvest. The climax of the growth is obvious. In the same way, we cannot tell from day to day what specific growth God may be seeing in us, but we trust the process. God will know when He has achieved His purpose in us. The Christian rests in the security of God's process. The harvest will come.

This world-view is characterized by self-discipline. It will sacrifice the pleasure of the moment for a higher value. It wants to spend time in prayer, Bible study, witness, and meditation. These are the exercises or disciplines that feed and flex the muscles of the soul.

The worldly view is dominated by self. It looks inward. All events and circumstances are evaluated according to their reward of self. Each particular individual with this world-view is at the center of his or her own universe. The people he or she encounters are useful or useless according to the need that self expresses. Events are evaluated according to their serviceability to the particular person.

The Christly world-view is dominated by love, first for God and then for others. Where the world is self-directed, the Christly is other-directed. Its look is either upward or outward. God is at the center of the universe for these people. People are valued because God loves them and because they are serving Him. Fellowship among believers takes on a richness because of the high love among them. Events assume deep meaning as God's reign is extended or perhaps vindicated by some noble sacrifice.

The worldly view is jealous when another succeeds. Yet love can share all of life with others—sorrows, achievements, setbacks, and progress. The joys of the Christly view are higher because the joys of others are its own. It appreciates the seriousness of another's problem or the elation of a goal met. Love lives for others.

Finally, the worldly view has a demonstrable horizon. Its goals are short term most of the time. It lives for the next sexual encounter, the next business success, the next career breakthrough. Even when it adopts long-term goals, success is temporal. It never sees beyond the grave. Indeed, many people see no point in looking beyond this life.

The Christly world-view has a cosmic horizon. Short-term goals are part of an immense picture that always includes eternity. Momentary defeat loses its sting because the preoccupation of the Christly person is with a broader canvas. The Christly mind wants to bring all of creation under the rulership of Christ. That overarching goal controls all the thinking within this world-view. The culmination in Christ's lordship is certain, and so all events leading to that consummation are minor in relation to the final momentous event.

I do not know when Christ will return, but while we are waiting my goal in life is to bring every creature to submit to His reign in their hearts. Right now that is the only place He can reign. We cannot make others submit to His rule, but we can make our goal to present Him in all His attractiveness to friend and foe, to the sensitive and insensitive, to unbelievers and believers. Our job is to make the kingdom within widespread. We are concerned about our own mind and want to help others have the mind of Christ. We hope many will share the blessing of the kingdom within.

The Kingdom Within Us

The individual with the kingdom within is blessed of God. The kingdom within blesses because it is the source of a deep and undisturbable happiness. The blessing has two main expressions.

The first is peace. We have seen repeatedly that the mind of Christ is an integrated mind, where every factor and facet work together instead of against each other. All parts of the mind are in harmony with one another. Because of that, outer conflict cannot penetrate the peace that makes up that harmony. Thousands of martyrs have gone to the gallows or to the stake with tranquility marking their face as a witness to their executioners.

This peace is both a gift and a discipline. The gift is the Holy Spirit's blessing on the integrated mind. The discipline is that self-control that will not allow foreign thoughts to disquiet the processes of thought. This does not mean that Satan cannot tempt. He can. He will often try to disturb the composure of the disciplined mind. Sometimes he succeeds. But since discipline is a fruit of the Spirit, Satan's success is not automatic. We can resist him with the power of the Spirit. Peace is the birthright of the believer and the fruit of the Spirit.

The second aspect of the blessing is joy. The highest joy that the redeemed individual can know is "the grace of the Lord Jesus Christ, and the love of God, and the fellowship of the Holy Spirit" (2 Cor. 13:14). Joy is also a gift and a discipline. This gift also is a fruit of the Spirit (Gal. 5:22). The discipline is abiding in Christ. After talking about abiding, He said, "These things I have spoken to you, that My joy may be in you, and that your joy may be made full" (John 15:11). We are to abide in Him to have the joy.

Do you have peace and joy? Below are the two world-views set out in parallel columns. These columns are ways of thinking. Prayerfully check the one on the left or the one on the right, according to which characterizes your own thoughts. At this point you may have some thought patterns that follow the left-hand side. When you honestly find yourself on that side, begin praying that God will move you to the right-hand side. Like all the exercises in this book, this should be done alone and in prayer.

Worldly View	Christly View
I was born unlucky (or lucky).	God has had His hand on me in the reading of this book.
I become bitter when one of my goals is frustrated.	In my setbacks, I reckon on God bringing a greater good than I could have known otherwise.
I am rarely aware that a blessing actually comes from God.	I am aware that all blessings come from above.
My sins continue to plague me; I find it hard to go on.	After I sin, I ask God's forgiveness and move on in the confidence that I am a product of the future.
I cannot tell that I am becoming anything.	I can perceive process and progress in God conforming me to the image of Christ
I live for the physical, whether it is sex, food, money, or position.	The values most important to me are definable but unseen, spiritual values.

I am a slave to my appetites.	My body is subject to my spirit. This may be expressed in my willingness to fast, pray, study, or witness.
My faith is controlled by what I can see.	I act on the belief that the physical world is under the control of the spiritual world.
My strength helps me meet the challenges of life.	I depend on the Holy Spirit to do everything I do.
I live for moments of gratification.	I live in a continuum of joy.
I am impulsive.	Although I have punctuation marks of joy or pain, my overall life continues to move toward the high calling of Christ Jesus.
I continue to grow more introspective as the years go by.	I find myself looking upward to God and outward to others more and more as the years go by.
My success is more important to me than anything else in the world.	I get a joy in helping others succeed.
I get jealous when something good happens to someone else.	I enjoy seeing good things happen to another person.
I cannot sympathize with another person's hurt.	I weep with those who weep.
My life is dominated by short-term goals.	All my goals are subservient to the life goal of bringing the world to the feet of Christ.
My horizon is limited by time.	The only horizon I have is eternity.
Physical death is the end of life.	Physical death is the beginning of real life.

I have tried to say that having the mind of Christ is a process. If you were totally honest with God as you took this test, you should be admitting that too much of you is on the left-hand side. This chapter and the right column of this test describe a world-view that you want to work toward. It will be work, a work of discipline and a work of prayer. Arriving completely on the right-hand side will be accomplished only over a period of time, through process. You want the same world-view that Jesus had when He walked the earth and that He has right now. Not all of the orientations in the right column above were His, because He never sinned. We approach the embracing of His world-view with a background of sin and redemption. That is why we depend completely on the Holy Spirit.

Having the mind of Christ makes a difference in my life. I have a different world-view, and I put that world-view into practice as I go through life. Those who weep will find me weeping with them. Those who succeed will be surprised at my sharing their joy. The church will know that I am different because I find practical ways to express love there. This lost world will not doubt that I am different from them, because they too will notice me reaching to them in some practical expression of love.

Those in crisis will be drawn to my peace. I will be able to bring peace because I have it to give and to demonstrate. I can dispense comfort to the hurting as the Holy Comforter flows through me. Those who are indifferent will discover the possibility of joy through me. In other words, the Christly mind will minister. The Christly world-view is not real unless it finds pragmatic expression. After all, real Christians are different.

Conclusion

To have the mind of Christ, I must have His world-view or His outlook on life in general. All the other aspects of His mind that I develop will conform to the larger picture of His world-view. I will realize His world-view in my mind only through process, discipline, and prayer. He helps me learn His world-view in His office as Savior. Only the redeemed can become like Him. His world-view directs my thoughts, decisions, and actions.

PART FOUR

Now and Forever, Amen

chapter thirteen

A Kingdom Present and to Come

hath given him a name above every name

*J*esus told His listeners in Palestine that the kingdom of heaven was "at hand" (Matt. 4:17). The kingdom was there in the fact that the King was present. He had superficial followers who would accept Him as long as He made no personal demands on their life. After He made those demands clear, the shallow followers deserted Him, but a small group remained loyal (John 6:59–68). They were subjects of the King. His kingship did not depend on the number of His subjects. He ruled in their hearts; they were obedient under all circumstances. The kingdom was present, then and there.

The good news Jesus preached was the news of the kingdom (Luke 8:1). This was the crux of His teaching. The happiest thing that could happen to the world would have been the visible manifestation of the kingdom in the obedience of Israel. To be obedient, the kingdom must first come in their hearts. That kingdom was available to anyone who would accept Him in their heart.

A Kingdom Present

The kingdom is present in the hearts of all believers. Paul wrote the Colossian church, "For He delivered us from the domain of darkness, and transferred us to the kingdom of His beloved Son" (Col. 1:13). Every

Christian has been delivered out of one realm, the realm of sin and darkness. We have been transferred into a different kingdom, the kingdom of light. That is where we live. The kingdom of Christ is a present reality.

What is this kingdom like? It has no earthly capital, no Washington or London or Tokyo. It is not proclaimed daily in the newspapers, as are the governments of this world. It receives very little recognition in the media of this age. Yet it has a government and a ruler. Its work is silent as far as the world is concerned and is visible only in the inner hearts and outer lives of its subjects.

Christ's kingdom endures. Earthly kingdoms rise and fall and move into oblivion. This is the story of nations and kingdoms from the beginning of recorded history. The kingdom of Christ has gone on for two thousand years. No enemy has been able to destroy it. During those millennia, it has grown and now claims subjects within every nation and culture.

The kingdom is not acultural but supracultural, above all earthly expressions of life. It transcends culture and can be expressed within any earthly culture. Culture never excludes anyone from the kingdom. Regardless of earthly language or expression, anyone can elect to become a citizen in the kingdom of heaven.

Peter says that this inner kingdom is an eternal kingdom (1 Pet. 1:11). It is indestructible from without. It will never decay from within because its author and ruler is eternal. What an assurance for those of us who are subjects in that kingdom.

It is a kingdom of light (Col. 1:13) and truth (John 18:37). Jesus connected His kingship with His nature as truth when He spoke to Pilate. No one in that kingdom need stumble, for they have light. They need not confuse right and wrong, for the King is Truth.

The kingdom has some surprising citizens. They are childlike. Jesus said, "Permit the children to come to Me; do not hinder them; for the kingdom of God belongs to such as these. Truly I say to you, whoever does not receive the kingdom of God like a child shall not enter it at all" (Mark 10:14–15). The poor are welcome in the kingdom (Luke 6:20). The kingdom is also for the poor in spirit and the persecuted (Matt. 5:3, 10). In God's kingdom, humility is of such value that most of this world will be shocked at the ranks assigned there.

The kingdom is of supreme value. No value on earth can compare with the worth of the kingdom of Christ. To show its value, He said,

"The kingdom of heaven is like a treasure hidden in the field, which a man found and hid; and from joy over it he goes and sells all that he has, and buys that field" (Matt. 13:44). Christ then compared it to a merchant who sold all he had to buy "one pearl of great value" (Matt. 13:45–46). All the treasures and values of earth fade into nothingness when compared with the value of Christ's kingdom.

Our present work is to extend the kingdom by all that is within our power. Jesus told us to pray, "Thy kingdom come" in the model prayer (Matt. 6:10). At present, we can only extend the kingdom within the hearts of men. We are broadening the kingdom within by our prayers and actions.

Our nature is to share the joy we have found with others. One way of sharing that joy is through fellowship with other believers. The church, as we have seen, is where "Christ in you" is expressed. He is also expressed as we tell the world about Him. Our commission is to take the good news to "the remotest part of the earth."

A Kingdom to Come

The kingdom not only is a present reality, some day it will come with power. Every spiritual Christian is waiting anxiously for the day when every knee shall bow. They will bow because that is the normal courtesy due a king. The Shekinah will return, and with it the universal reign of Christ. For subjects in that kingdom, that will be the happiest day in all of history.

In the Lord's Supper, Jesus told the disciples, "But I say to you, I will not drink of this fruit of the vine from now on until that day when I drink it new with you in My Father's kingdom" (Matt. 26:29). This implies some sort of celebration in that great climax of history. Those of us who have already bowed the knee will celebrate a feast that we cannot presently imagine.

John heard the loud voice in heaven proclaim, "The kingdom of the world has become the kingdom of our Lord, and of His Christ, and He will reign forever and ever" (Rev. 11:15). The voice equated the kingdom of our Lord with that of His Christ. The two are one kingdom, and that kingdom will embrace all of creation. All will bow to Christ, whether reluctantly or joyfully.

For the subjects of the kingdom, no happier destiny could be described than the description of Christ as He spoke of "the end of the age" (Matt. 13:39). He said of His own people, "Then the righteous will shine forth as the sun in the kingdom of their Father" (Matt. 13:43). What kind of eyes will God equip us with that we can behold one another in that kind of light?

So we live in a present kingdom, and we expect a future one to be unlimited. The factor common to both kingdoms is the presence of the king. He rules over some of us now, and some day all of creation will bow to Him. Isaiah said of the Messiah, "And the government will rest on His shoulders" (Isa. 9:6). In the next verse he said, "There will be no end to the increase of His government or of peace." This was what the Old Testament prophets expected. The King would govern.

Jesus told Pilate, "You say correctly that I am a king" (John 18:37). We now know that king in our hearts, and we will know Him in fuller dimensions at the end of the age. To know Him is to enjoy His presence. He promised us, "I am with you always, even to the end of the age" (Matt. 28:20).

At the end of the age, "These will wage war against the Lamb, and the Lamb will overcome them, because He is Lord of lords and King of kings" (Rev. 17:14). This is why we worship Christ and do not worship man. He and only He is Lord of all lords and King of all kings. Final victory is assured because of that. Our faith is secure because He is sovereign now and will be shown to be sovereign then.

If we seem to live in conflict now, victory is still assured. He is with us, and He is sovereign. We live victorious over circumstances, over enemies, and over the world. Victory is the possession of every believer in Christ.

Victory in Christ

All of God's saints through the centuries have been engaged in various battles of a long war. The final outcome of the war is assured and is spelled out in the Book of Revelation. God and His saints will conquer Satan. The war is decided but the battles continue, and we are in their midst.

We are deceived if we do not take into account that "our struggle is not against flesh and blood, but against the rulers, against the powers, against the world forces of this darkness, against the spiritual forces of wickedness in the heavenly places" (Eph. 6:12). With the spiritual armor of Ephesians 6:13–18, we are to "fight the good fight of faith" (1 Tim. 6:12). At the end of his life Paul claimed, "I have fought the good fight, I have finished the course, I have kept the faith" (2 Tim. 4:7). He finished victoriously, and so can we.

The battles we fight are in the arena of the mind. Here is where Satan and his forces work most tenaciously. When Jesus knew the thoughts of the Pharisees, He said, "The good man out of his good treasure brings forth what is good; and the evil man out of his evil treasure brings forth what is evil" (Matt. 12:35). We deceive ourselves if we do not understand that having the mind of Christ will involve struggle.

Paul shows that the struggle is in the mind when he writes, "For the weapons of our warfare are not of the flesh, but divinely powerful for the destruction of fortresses. We are destroying speculations and every lofty thing raised up against the knowledge of God, and we are taking every thought captive to the obedience of Christ" (2 Cor. 10:4–5).

Several years ago, during a particularly hard struggle, I stopped praising the Lord. For five days I brooded, then on the fifth day it occurred to me that when you praise the Lord on the mountaintop but refuse to praise Him in the valley, you are not praising the Lord, you are praising your feelings.

I did not feel like it, but in the strength of Christ I took possession of my thoughts and began praising the Lord in spite of my depression. His worth does not depend on our moods. It is a constant. I discovered that day a new definition for praise: praise is insisting on the truth. Truth as a person is invariable.

I vowed that day that I would never again let my feelings dictate my awareness of my position in Christ. Our position is not a product of our feelings. Christ's victory is eternal, a constant, independent of our emotions.

Our present responsibility is to fight our battles in the spirit of Jesus. What Jahaziel told Jehoshaphat applies to all time: "The battle is not yours but God's" (2 Chron. 20:15). The New Testament consistently speaks of victory, not as something we accomplish, but as the appropriation of what Jesus has already accomplished.

Paul proclaimed, "But thanks be to God, who always leads us in His triumph in Christ, and manifests through us the sweet aroma of the knowledge of Him in every place" (2 Cor. 2:14). Victory is not an outcome to be achieved, but steps to follow. When we walk in Christ and He alone is shown and exalted in our life, we are already in victory.

John spoke of vanquishing the world: "You are from God, little children, and have overcome them; because greater is He who is in you than he who is in the world" (1 John 4:4). For the spiritual Christian, victory is not an event, but the victor abiding in us.

He further says, "For whatever is born of God overcomes the world; and this is the victory that has overcome the world—our faith. And who is the one who overcomes the world, but he who believes that Jesus is the Son of God?" (1 John 5:4–5). The proof of faith is not in success or even in answered prayer, but in enduring.

We do not have the privilege of giving up or acquiescing to Satan. Since the battle is not ours but God's, we are not the ones to make that choice. Paul urged Timothy, "Suffer hardship with me, as a good soldier of Christ Jesus" (2 Tim. 2:3). Moses persevered "as seeing Him who is unseen" (Heb. 11:27).

All spiritual forces are subject to Christ. The demons had to obey Him because He had authority. His final victory is the inevitable result of the work of the cross. When the forces of evil succeeded in pinning the incarnate second person of the Trinity to the cross, they thought they had defeated God. But that cross proved to be their undoing. "When He had disarmed the rulers and authorities, He made a public display of them, having triumphed over them through Him" (Col. 2:15). Victory is not justice waiting to be accomplished, but a debt that has been fully paid.

The final enemy to be vanquished is death itself. The finality of death, the real meaning of death, will be realized for the unbeliever ultimately in what the Bible calls the second death (Rev. 20:14). But for the believer, "When this perishable will have put on the imperishable, and this mortal will have put on immortality, then will come about the saying that is written, 'Death is swallowed up in victory. O death, where is your victory? O death, where is your sting?' The sting of death is sin, and the power of sin is the law; but thanks be to God, who gives us the victory through our Lord Jesus Christ" (1 Cor. 15:54–57).

For believers, death is momentary, a passage into the presence of Christ. Death is the path to full knowledge and the end of Satan's obstruction of our understanding. God here manifests His final victory after having indwelt our life of struggle. Beyond death is the reward we were seeking as we grappled with the forces of the world. Passing through this doorway, we at last fully appropriate safety and eternal sanctuary. For the Christian, real death (eternal, not momentary) happened on the cross of Christ. I died, was crucified, with Christ two thousand years ago. We do not dread the past.

"Nay, in all these things we are more than conquerors through him that loved us" (Rom. 8:37 KJV). How can you be more than a conqueror? Imagine a kingdom being invaded by foreign forces. The king sends his most outstanding general with his finest troops to fight the invader. The general routs the enemy and sends them scurrying back to their country. The general is now the conqueror and great tribute would be given him. But who is greater than the conqueror? The only person in the kingdom who is greater than the conqueror is the king himself. What is more than a conqueror? A ruler. We who will reign with Christ are "more than conquerors."

Do not be surprised if Satan tries to thwart you in your effort to live by the principles of this book. Christ never promised that living His life would be easy. In one aspect of our position in Christ, the battles are already won. We have the mind of Christ, and our problem is only how to realize it in the context of a difficult and hindering world. But being in that world is the other aspect of our position in Christ. Realizing that mind may be a problem and even a battle at times. Nevertheless, always remember that you had the mind of Christ even at spiritual birth. That baby mind in us must grow, and the growth process is beset by the habits of our old sin nature, the obstruction of Satan, and the appeal of the world.

Victory is ours. Our triumph was accomplished two thousand years ago when Christ fully satisfied the dread and holy requirements of God on the cross, conquered death, and ascended to intercede for us until the final battle is won. Jesus is the Lord of lords and the King of kings. He is our high priest who intercedes for us. He has been interceding for you even as you have read this book. He will continue to intercede for you as you grow in His likeness and as you demonstrate His likeness to your fellow creatures. Victory is being like Jesus Christ. That is our destiny.

Conclusion

I was created to be like Jesus Christ. He is in me and remains with me always. He is my present King, and one day every knee will bow to Him as sovereign. In all that I do and say, I represent Him to my fellow man. In whatever struggle I face, I know that He is with me and the victory is assured because the battle is not mine but His. He assures my victory in His office as Lord of lords and King of kings.

A small group workbook,
The Mind of Christ,
by T.W. Hunt and Claude V. King
is available from

The Baptist Sunday School Board
127 Ninth Avenue North
Nashville, TN 37234

Notes

Chapter 1 — The Mind of Christ

1. Concerning this passage as a hymn, see Richard R. Melick, *Philippians, Colossians, Philemon,* The New American Commentary, vol. 32 (Nashville: Broadman Press, 1991), 96–97.

Chapter 4 — The Lifestyle of Christ

1. A friend asked me to use the word *pharisaical* rather than *puritanical* because of the healthy contribution of the Puritans to Christian history. Although I agree that we all need to learn from the Puritans, *pharisaical* is not in common usage among most people. I prefer to stick to the commonly understood term *puritanical.* The *real* Puritans were not puritanical.

Chapter 7 — A Man

1. "Completeness, wholeness, harmony, fulfillment, are closer to the meaning [of the Hebrew word for peace, *shalom*]," R. Laird Harris, Gleason L. Archer, and Bruce K. Waltkie, *Theological Word Book of the Old Testament* (Chicago: Moody Press, 1980), 2:931.

Chapter 9 — Crucified

1. For this one chapter, unless otherwise noted, the scriptural material comes from Matthew 26:30–27:56; Mark 14:32–15:41; Luke 22:39–23:49; and John 18:1–19:37. Because the majority of the material in this chapter comes directly from these Scriptures and because of the abundance of footnotes on the legal and medical aspects of the crucifixion, the only Scripture that I have noted is to direct quotations and material not directly from the crucifixion passages in an attempt to improve the readability of the account. In a few cases I have combined words and phrases from two of the Gospels to give a complete account. The chronology is that of A. T. Robertson, *A Harmony of the Gospels for Students of the Life of Christ* (New York: Harper & Row, 1922), 201–35. If you would like to locate a given

incident quickly, consult Robert L. Thomas and Stanley N. Gundry, *A Harmony of the Gospels with Explanations and Essays* (Chicago: Moody Press, 1978), 221–49. The Thomas-Gundry harmony follows the chronology of Robertson. To comprehend the flow of the events in this chapter and the next and to understand their significance, I recommend that you first read the accounts without consulting the footnotes. For further study, reread the chapters consulting the notes.

2. William D. Edwards, Wesley J. Gabel, Floyd E. Hosmer, "On the Physical Death of Jesus Christ," *Journal of the American Medical Association* 255, no. 11, March 21, 1986, 1456; used with permission from the Mayo Foundation. Many commentators believe the reference is to profuse perspiration rather than hematidrosis. Luke (22:44) says, "And being in agony He was praying very fervently; and His sweat became like [or as] drops of blood, falling down upon the ground" (*kai egeneto ho hidros autou hosei thromboi haimatos katabainontes epi ten gen*). However, most medical authorities who have written on the subject believe that His later weakness—unusual for Him—is an indication that He did indeed sweat blood prior to the trials. His rapid death also indicates forces that weakened Him before the later ordeals. Death by crucifixion normally came slowly, sometimes after several days. See Joel B. Green, "Death of Jesus," in *Dictionary of Jesus and the Gospels,* edited by Joel B. Green and Scot McKnight (Downers Grove, Ill.: InterVarsity Press, 1992), 147. Jesus' body was probably unusually strong at the beginning of the ordeals, and yet He expired quickly, almost too quickly for a normal crucifixion. Each phase of the ordeal was more traumatic than is generally known.

3. C. Truman Davis, "The Crucifixion of Jesus: The Passion of Christ from a Medical Point of View," *Arizona Medicine* (March 1965): 184.

4. Louis A. Barbieri, Jr., "That Incredible Mistrial," *Moody Monthly,* April 1973, 44. In Acts 24:1–9, Tertullus accused Paul, but Tertullus was probably not a Jew and the court was Roman, not Jewish.

5. For information on Jewish witnesses, see Walter M. Chandler, *The Trial of Jesus from a Lawyer's Standpoint* (Norcross, Ga.: Harrison Co., 1976), 64–75; and Dale Foreman, *Crucify Him: A Lawyer Looks at the Trial of Jesus* (Grand Rapids, Mich.: Zondervan, 1990), 116–18. For the sake of space, in this account I have not dwelt on the many important legal violations in Jesus' various trials. Consult the above books. See also the Barbieri article in the note 4, 41–46.

6. Some authorities think that Roman legionnaires accompanied the priests and Pharisees to arrest Jesus. See David Smith, *The Days of His Flesh: The Earthly Life of Our Lord and Savior Jesus Christ* (1905; reprint, Grand Rapids, Mich.: Baker, 1976), 458; and Jim Bishop, *The Day Christ Died* (New York: Harper & Row, 1957), 193.

7. Bishop, *The Day Christ Died,* 201. Bishop thinks it may have been as late as 4:00 A.M. In view of all that was yet to occur before the crucifixion, a somewhat earlier hour seems likely to me. Following the Robertson and

Thomas-Gundry harmonies, this trial was held illegally in a private home, Caiaphas's house (Luke 22:54).

8. *Wycliffe Bible Encyclopedia,* s.v. "Sanhedrin." A trial at night was obviously illegal. The official Sanhedrin could not try a court on a feast day, nor were courts to meet until after the morning prayer and sacrifice. See Barbieri, "That Incredible Mistrial," 42–44.

9. Throughout this trial and the trial in Caiaphas's house, Judas is nowhere to be seen. Robertson and the Thomas-Gundry harmonies place Judas's remorse and suicide after Jesus' formal condemnation in the morning trial by the Sanhedrin. Indeed, this is where Matthew places it. The morning trial is recorded in Matthew 27:1 and Judas's suicide follows that. Although he absented himself during the night trial in Caiaphas's house, Judas probably attended the morning session of the Sanhedrin. Once Jesus confessed His messiahship (Matt. 26:64; Mark 14:62), Judas's witness would no longer be needed. Judas committed suicide after he "saw that He had been condemned" (Matt. 27:3).

10. Foreman, *Crucify Him,* 117.

11. Barbieri, "That Incredible Mistrial," 44.

12. Foreman, *Crucify Him,* 118.

13. Paul L. Maier, *First Easter: The True and Unfamiliar Story in Word and Picture* (New York: Harper & Row, 1973), 48. Various traditions had sprung up that actually invalidated the Levitical law. An example of a tradition that contravened the law may be seen in Matthew 15:1–9.

14. Robert Duncan Culver, *The Life of Christ* (Grand Rapids, Mich.: Baker, 1976), 244.

15. Chandler, *Trial of Jesus,* 59. Josh McDowell, in *The Resurrection Factor* (San Bernardino, Calif.: Here's Life, 1981), 41, states that the Sanhedrin of seventy -one could not try a case involving capital punishment. Therefore this was probably the smaller Sanhedrin of twenty-three members.

16. Chandler, *Trial of Jesus,* 77, 128–129.

17. Culver, *Life of Christ,* 244.

18. Smith, *Days of His Flesh,* 472.

19. Chandler, *Trial of Jesus,* 90.

20. Foreman, *Crucify Him,* 132.

21. Davis, "Crucifixion of Jesus," 184.

22. Maier, *First Easter,* 68.

23. *The International Standard Bible Encyclopedia,* s.v. "Cross, Crucify."

24. *Theological Dictionary of the New Testament,* s.v. "Mastigoo, Mastizo, Mastiz."

25. Alice N. Pohl, "Did Jesus Get a Fair Trial?" *Moody Monthly,* April 1982, 16.

26. Edwards, Gabel, and Hosmer, "On the Physical Death of Jesus Christ," 1457; see also Smith, *Days of His Flesh,* 487.

27. Schneider, 519.

28. Smith, *Days of His Flesh,* 487.

29. Edwards, Gabel, and Hosmer, "On the Physical Death of Jesus Christ," 1457.

30. Davis, "Crucifixion of Jesus," 185.

31. Smith, *Days of His Flesh*, 487.

32. David Dunavant, "A Christian Physician Explains the Death of Jesus Christ," *Baptist Record*, April 15, 1976, 3. Dunavant's study is found in two parts in the April 8, 1976 and April 15, 1976 issues of the *Baptist Record*. The same study is available in an unpublished monograph and a tape recording that can be ordered from Bellevue Baptist Church, Memphis, Tennessee.

33. Edwards, Gabel, and Hosmer, "On the Physical Death of Jesus Christ," 1457.

34. Ibid., 1458.

35. Ibid., 1457.

36. Bishop, *The Day Christ Died*, 41–42; see also J. Dwight Pentecost, *The Words and Works of Jesus Christ: A Study of the Life of Christ* (Grand Rapids, Mich.: Zondervan, 1981), 476.

37. Will Durant, *Caesar and Christ: A History of Roman Civilization and of Christianity from Their Beginnings to A.D. 325,* The Story of Civilization, vol. 3 (New York: Simon and Schuster, 1944), 264. For an interesting treatment of this episode, see Paul L. Maier, *Pontius Pilate* (Wheaton, Ill.: Tyndale, 1970), 156–61. Although this is a documented historical, biblical novel, Maier is known for scrupulous scholarship and has published numerous scholarly monographs on this biblical period. He notes that his information on Sejanus comes primarily from Dio Cassius, 58.9ff. He also references Suetonius, *Tiberius*, 60, and Seneca, *De Tranquillate Animi*, 11.11.

38. A. T. Robertson, *Studies in the New Testament* (Nashville, Tenn.: Sunday School Board of the Southern Baptist Convention, 1915), 21.

39. Maier, *First Easter*, 73; see also Maier, *Pontius Pilate*, 43.

40. Flavius Josephus, *The Jewish War* (*De bello Judaico*), ed. Gaalya Cornfeld (Grand Rapids, Mich.: Zondervan, 1982), 156, n. 177.

41. Josephus, *The Jewish War*, 155–56.

42. Ibid., 156.

43. Maier, *First Easter*, 65.

44. Pierre Barbet, *A Doctor at Calvary: The Passion of Our Lord Jesus Christ as Described by a Surgeon,* trans. the Earl of Wicklow (New York: Image Books, 1963), 38. The original edition was published in French in 1950. Although Barbet bases his primary studies of Jesus' physical sufferings on the shroud of Turin, his medical and historical researches are thoroughly documented.

45. Edwards, Gabel, and Hosmer, "On the Physical Death of Jesus Christ," 1458.

46. Barbet, *Doctor at Calvary*, 47.

47. Edwards, Gabel, and Hosmer, "On the Physical Death of Jesus Christ," 1459.

48. Edward R. Bloomquist, "A Doctor Looks at the Crucifixion," *Christian Herald*, March 1964, 47.

49. Matt. 27:34; Mark 15:23. On the Jewish women, see Bishop, *The Day Christ Died*, 272, 277–78.

50. Edwards, Gabel, and Hosmer, "On the Physical Death of Jesus Christ," 1462.

51. Robert Wassener, "A Physician Looks at the Suffering Christ," *Moody Monthly*, March 1979, 42. See also Bloomquist, "A Doctor Looks," 48.

52. These facts are deduced from the ossuary remains of a first-century tomb of a crucifixion victim unearthed at Giv'at ha-Mivtar in 1968. See *The International Standard Bible Encyclopedia,* s.v. "Cross, Crucify"; and Edwards, Gabel, and Hosmer, "On the Physical Death of Jesus Christ," 1459. See also Bloomquist, "A Doctor Looks," 48. Bloomquist's article was written before the discovery of the remains of the crucifixion victim.

53. Wassener, "Physician Looks at the Suffering Christ," 42.

54. *Wycliffe Bible Encyclopedia,* s.v. "cross."

55. Marcus L. Loane, *The Place Called Calvary* (Grand Rapids, Mich.: Zondervan, 1956, 1968), 49.

56. Bloomquist, "A Doctor Looks," 48.

57. Edwards, Gable, and Hosmer, "On the Physical Death of Jesus Christ," 1461.

58. *Wycliffe Bible Encyclopedia,* s.v. "cross"; and Edwards, Gable, and Hosmer, "On the Physical Death of Jesus Christ," 1461.

59. See Wassener, "Physician Looks at the Suffering Christ," 42, and Dunavant, "Christian Physician Explains the Death of Christ," 2.

60. Edwards, Gable, and Hosmer, "On the Physical Death of Jesus Christ," 1460–61; see also Dunavant, "Christian Physician Explains the Death of Christ," 3.

61. Wassener, "Physician Looks at the Suffering Christ," 42; see also Barbet, *Doctor at Calvary,* 108.

62. Bloomquist, "A Doctor Looks," 48.

63. Martin Hengel, *Crucifixion,* trans. John Bowden (Philadelphia: Fortress Press, 1977), 3.

64. Ibid., 37.

65. Barbet, *Doctor at Calvary,* 201; see also Davis, "Crucifixion of Jesus," 186.

66. Foreman, *Crucify Him,* 139; and *The International Standard Bible Encyclopedia,* s.v. "Cross, Crucify."

67. Bloomquist, "A Doctor Looks," 48.

68. Davis, "Crucifixion of Jesus," 187.

69. I am aware that some theologians do not accept this separation of Father from Son at this point. But many reliable ones do. Having studied and prayed about the cross for more than thirty years, I am convinced that the separation at this point had to be. If Jesus had not known this dread exile from God, He would neither have suffered the seriousness of our sin nor would He have appeased the holiness of God. Hell is not hell if there is no separation from God. His cry, "My God, My God, why hast Thou forsaken Me?" (Mark 15:34) would have had no meaning without the separation. That cry validates the truth of the separation.

70. Quoted by William R. Nicholson, *The Six Miracles of Calvary* (Chicago: Moody Press, 1928), 20.

71. See Bishop, *The Day Christ Died,* 303, note 35.

72. Culver, *Life of Christ,* 257.

73. Dunavant, "Christian Physician Explains the Death of Christ," 3. Dr. Ernest Byers suggested in a September 21, 1993, letter to me that with all that Jesus

had been subjected to, plus the significant time interval, this dilation may have resulted from a stress ulcer of the stomach that perforated the stomach wall, dumping blood, gastric juices, and even bile into the abdominal cavity. Normally, under the severity of the trauma, especially considering the fact of the enormous sin Jesus was carrying, a person would lose consciousness. Since He evidently did not lose consciousness, the extreme stress could have produced an ulcer.

74. Davis, "Crucifixion of Jesus," 187.
75. Ibid.; see John 19:29.
76. On the fact that He willed His death, see Loane, *Place Called Calvary,* 127–28.

Chapter 10—Raised from the Dead

1. Again in this chapter the only Scriptures I cite are direct quotations. The scriptural material comes from Matthew 27:57–28:20, Mark 15:42–16:8, Luke 23:50–24:53, John 19:31–21:25, Acts 1:12, and 1 Corinthians 15:5–7. A given incident can be located quickly by consulting the Thomas-Gundry harmony. I accept the Robertson and Thomas-Gundry conclusion that the appearance in Matthew 28:16–20 is the same as that mentioned in 1 Corinthians 15:6.
2. Edersheim, *The Life and Times of Jesus the Messiah* (1882; reprint, Grand Rapids, Mich.: Eerdmans, 1974), 2:611; see also the elaborate description of the Holy Place and the Holy of Holies in Josephus, *The Jewish War,* 358–60. There the height of the Holy of Holies is also given as twenty cubits, or about thirty feet.
3. Bishop, *The Day Christ Died,* 211.
4. *The International Standard Bible Encyclopedia,* s.v. "Cross, Crucify."
5. Barbet, *Doctor at Calvary,* 138, 143.
6. Ibid., 138.
7. Dunavant, "Christian Physician Explains the Death of Christ," 3. Blood would also have been in the abdominal cavity if a stress ulcer had developed during the trauma. See note 73 of chapter 10.
8. Edwin A. Blum, "John," in John F. Walvoord and Roy B. Zuck, eds., *The Life of Christ Commentary* (Wheaton, Ill.: Victor Books, 1989), 341.
9. Bishop, *The Day Christ Died,* 291.
10. J. Dwight Pentecost, *The Words and Works of Jesus Christ, A Study of the Life of Christ* (Grand Rapids, Mich.: Zondervan, 1981), 501.
11. Edersheim, *Life and Times,* 618.
12. Barbet, *Doctor at Calvary,* 161.
13. Ibid., 163, 169; see also Maier, *First Easter,* 91.
14. Maier, *First Easter,* 91.
15. Ibid., 117.
16. Bishop, *The Day Christ Died,* 298.
17. Edersheim, *Life and Times,* 618.

18. For a popular treatment of this well-known Jewish fact, see Martha Zimmerman, *Celebrate the Feasts of the Old Testament in Your Own Home or Church* (Minneapolis: Bethany House, 1981), 32.

19. Mark says that Mary Magdalene, Mary the Mother of James and Joses, and Salome, plus "many other women who had come up with Him to Jerusalem" were at the cross (Mark 15:40–41). Luke adds the name of Joanna, the wife of Herod's steward Chuza, as being present at the discovery of the empty tomb (24:10). He also states that "the women who accompanied Him from Galilee" were at the cross (Luke 23:49). This would certainly have included Susanna (Luke 8:3). Mark listed the most prominent women; his addition of "many" others surely would mean at least five or six, two of whose names are known. This would probably make about eight or nine women.

20. See Culver, *Life of Christ*, 268.

21. On these words, see E. L. C. Austin, *Earth's Greatest Day* (Grand Rapids, Mich.: Baker, 1979), 43.

22. See the second meaning of *airo* in Joseph Henry Thayer, *Greek-English Lexicon of the New Testament* (Grand Rapids, Mich.: Zondervan, 1962), 16; see also the discussion of *airo* in Ethelbert W. Bullinger, *A Critical Lexicon and Concordance to the English and Greek New Testament* (Grand Rapids, Mich.: Zondervan, 1975), 756. Mary's whole concern was with the whereabouts of the body. Her fearful complaint to Simon and John was, "We do not know where they have laid Him!" (John 20:2).

23. Austin, *Earth's Greatest Day*, 48.

24. Maier, *First Easter*, 98, states that the testimony of women would be deemed unreliable.

25. This is a personal opinion. The phrase in the King James Version in Matthew 28:9, "And as they went to tell his disciples," is not contained in the best manuscripts and is omitted from the NASB and the NIV. The women obviously were on their way somewhere, although the Bible does not indicate where. The best supposition seems to be that they were simply bewildered—the men refused to believe them—and they needed to retrace their steps to reassure themselves of the emptiness of the tomb.

26. Bullinger, *Lexicon and Concordance*, 349; see also the discussion in Austin, *Earth's Greatest Day*, 74.

27. Fritz Rienecker, *A Linguistic Key to the Greek New Testament*, ed. by Cleon L. Rogers Jr. (Grand Rapids, Mich.: Zondervan, 1976), 214; see also the discussion in Raymond Brown, "An Unusual Easter Miracle," in Gavin Reid, ed., *The Empty Cross: Ten Leading Christians Speak about the Cross and Resurrection of Christ* (Eastbourne: Kingsway, 1989), 71.

28. See the discussions of hallucinations in Maier, *First Easter*, 112–13, and Nelson L. Price, *The Destruction of Death* (Nashville, Tenn.: Broadman Press, 1982), 70–71. For a complete discussion of all objections to the resurrection (very important, but outside the scope of what I am trying to accomplish), see McDowell, *The Resurrection Factor*.

Bibliography

Books

Austin, E. L. C. *Earth's Greatest Day.* Grand Rapids, Mich.: Baker, 1979.

Barbet, Pierre. *A Doctor at Calvary: The Passion of our Lord Jesus Christ as Described by a Surgeon.* Translated by the Earl of Wicklow. New York: Image Books, 1963.

Bishop, Jim. *The Day Christ Died.* New York: Harper & Row, 1957.

Bullinger, Ethelbert W. *A Critical Lexicon and Concordance to the English and Greek New Testament.* Grand Rapids, Mich.: Zondervan, 1975.

Chandler, Walter M. *The Trial of Jesus from a Lawyer's Standpoint.* Norcross, Ga.: Harrison Co., 1976.

Culver, Robert Duncan. *The Life of Christ.* Grand Rapids, Mich.: Baker, 1976.

Durant, Will. *Caesar and Christ: A History of Roman Civilization and of Christianity from Their Beginnings to A.D. 325.* The Story of Civilization, vol. 3. New York: Simon and Schuster, 1944.

Edersheim, Alfred. *The Life and Times of Jesus the Messiah.* 1882; reprint, Grand Rapids, Mich.: Eerdmans, 1974.

Foreman, Dale. *Crucify Him: A Lawyer Looks at the Trial of Jesus.* Grand Rapids, Mich.: Zondervan, 1990.

Green, Joel B. and Scot McKnight. *Dictionary of Jesus and the Gospels.* Downers Grove, Ill.: InterVarsity Press, 1992.

Hengel, Martin. *Crucifixion.* Translated by John Bowden. Philadelphia: Fortress Press, 1977.

Hunt, T. W. *The Doctrine of Prayer.* Nashville, Tenn.: Convention Press, 1986.

Josephus, Flavius. *The Jewish War (De bello Judaico).* Edited by Gaalya Cornfeld. Grand Rapids, Mich.: Zondervan, 1982.

Loane, Marcus L. *The Place Called Calvary.* Grand Rapids, Mich.: Zondervan, 1956, 1968.

Maier, Paul L. *First Easter: The True and Unfamiliar Story in Word and Picture.* New York: Harper & Row, 1973.

———. *Pontius Pilate.* Wheaton, Ill.: Tyndale, 1970.

McDowell, Josh. *The Resurrection Factor.* San Bernardino, Calif.: Here's Life, 1981.

Melick, Richard R. *Philippians, Colossians, Philemon.* The New American Commentary. Vol. 32. Nashville, Tenn.: Broadman Press, 1991.

Morris, Leon. *The Gospel According to St. Luke: An Introduction and Commentary.* The Tyndale New Testament Commentaries. Vol. 3. Grand Rapids, Mich.: Eerdmans, 1974 .

Nicholson, William R. *The Six Miracles of Calvary.* Chicago: Moody Press, 1928.

Pentecost, J. Dwight. *The Words and Works of Jesus Christ, a Study of the Life of Christ.* Grand Rapids, Mich.: Zondervan, 1981.

Price, Nelson L. *The Destruction of Death.* Nashville, Tenn.: Broadman Press, 1982.

Rienecker, Fritz. *A Linguistic Key to the Greek New Testament.* Translated by Cleon L. Rogers Jr. Grand Rapids, Mich.: Zondervan, 1976.

Robertson, A. T. *A Harmony of the Gospels for Students of the Life of Christ.* New York: Harper & Row, 1922.

———. *Studies in the New Testament.* Nashville, Tenn.: Sunday School Board of the Southern Baptist Convention, 1915.

Schilder, Klaas. *Christ on Trial.* Grand Rapids, Mich.: Baker, 1939.

Smith, David. *The Days of His Flesh: The Earthly Life of Our Lord and Savior Jesus Christ.* 1905. Reprint. Grand Rapids, Mich.: Baker, 1976.

Thayer, Joseph Henry. *Greek-English Lexicon of the New Testament.* Grand Rapids, Mich.: Zondervan, 1962.

Thomas, Robert L. and Stanley N. Gundry. *A Harmony of the Gospels with Explanations and Essays.* Chicago: Moody Press, 1978.

Warfield, Benjamin Breckinridge. *The Person and Work of Christ.* Grand Rapids, Mich.: Baker, 1950.

Zimmerman, Martha. *Celebrate the Feasts of the Old Testament in Your Own Home or Church.* Minneapolis: Bethany House Publishers, 1981.

Articles

Barbieri, Louis A., Jr. "That Incredible Mistrial." *Moody Monthly,* April 1973.

Bloomquist, Edward R. "A Doctor Looks at the Crucifixion." *Christian Herald,* March 1964.

Blum, Edwin A. "John." In John F. Walvoord and Roy B. Zuck, eds., *The Life of Christ Commentary.* Wheaton, Victor Books, 1989.

Brown, Raymond. "An Unusual Easter Miracle." *The Empty Cross: Ten Leading Christians Speak about the Cross and Resurrection of Christ.* Edited by Gavin Reid. Eastbourne: Kingsway, 1989.

Davis, C. Truman. "The Crucifixion of Jesus: The Passion of Christ from a Medical Point of View." *Arizona Medicine,* March 1965.

Dunavant, David. "A Christian Physician Explains the Death of Jesus Christ." *Baptist Record,* April 8, 1976, 1–2, and April 15, 1976, 1, 3.

Edwards, William D., Wesley J. Gabel, and Floyd E. Hosmer. "On the Physical Death of Jesus Christ." *Journal of the American Medical Association* 255, no. 11, March 21, 1986; used with permission from the Mayo Foundation.

The International Standard Bible Encyclopedia. S.v. "Cross, Crucify."

Pohl, Alice N. "Did Jesus Get a Fair Trial?" *Moody Monthly,* April 1982.

Theological Dictionary of the New Testament. S.v. "Mastigoo, Mastizo, Mastiz."

Wassener, Robert. "A Physician Looks at the Suffering Christ." *Moody Monthly,* March 1979.

Wycliffe Bible Encyclopedia. S.v. "cross," "Sanhedrin."

STEPS TO PEACE WITH GOD

1. RECOGNIZE GOD'S PLAN—PEACE AND LIFE

The message you have read in this book stresses that God loves you and wants you to experience His peace and life.

The BIBLE says . . . *"For God loved the world so much that He gave His only Son, so that everyone who believes in Him may not die but have eternal life." John 3:16*

2. REALIZE OUR PROBLEM—SEPARATION

People choose to disobey God and go their own way. This results in separation from God.

The BIBLE says . . . *"Everyone has sinned and is far away from God's saving presence." Romans 3:23*

3. RESPOND TO GOD'S REMEDY—CROSS OF CHRIST

God sent His Son to bridge the gap. Christ did this by paying the penalty of our sins when He died on the cross and rose from the grave.

The BIBLE says . . . *"But God has shown us how much He loves us—it was while we were still sinners that Christ died for us!" Romans 5:8*

4. RECEIVE GOD'S SON—LORD AND SAVIOR

You cross the bridge into God's family when you ask Christ to come into your life.

The BIBLE says . . . *"Some, however, did receive Him and believed in Him; so He gave them the right to become God's children." John 1:12*

THE INVITATION IS TO:
REPENT (turn from your sins) and by faith RECEIVE Jesus Christ into your heart and life and follow Him in obedience as your Lord and Savior.

PRAYER OF COMMITMENT
"Lord Jesus, I know I am a sinner. I believe You died for my sins. Right now, I turn from my sins and open the door of my heart and life. I receive You as my personal Lord and Savior. Thank You for saving me now. Amen."

If you want further help in the decision you have made, write to:
Billy Graham Evangelistic Association, P.O. Box 779, Minneapolis, MN 55440-0779